# Almost Rich

Lessons from the Bible Richest Woman who

never was

# Dr. Matthew Omondiale

E-Book ISBN: 978-1-969066-35-1

Paperback ISBN: 978-1-969066-36-8

Hardcover ISBN: 978-1-969066-37-5


Published by:
Columbus Book Publishers
www.columbusbookpublishers.com


Printed in the United States of America

# Dedication

*This book is dedicated to all Christians who desire to make money, be free from debts, and enjoy life. And to my sons Wealth Odianose Lumiphakade Omondiale and Shephard Ojeaga Singabenkosi Omondiale.*

# Acknowledgment

*My acknowledgement goes to my wife and mother of my sons, Pastor Mrs. S'phindile Immaculate Omondiale, and Mr. Kaifa Tulay for his input to this project.*

# About the Author

Dr. Matthew Omondiale is an ordained minister with Church of God Mission International, a passionate father, and a dedicated life coach. Amongst others, He is a certified counselor and a dynamic public speaker known for delivering impactful results. A graduate of Political Science from Ambrose Alli University, Dr. Omondiale also holds a Bachelor's degree in Theology and an honorary Doctorate of Divinity from Real Success Bible School, an affiliate of Harvest Bible University, USA.

He serves as an Ambassador of Peace with the United Peace Federation, committed to fostering unity and transformation in communities. Dr. Omondiale is anointed for such a time as this—empowered to inspire, uplift, and guide individuals toward purposeful living.

# Table of Contents

# Preface

Dear reader,

Having this book in your hand is the beginning of many supernatural happenings in your life, especially in the area of finances. I am privileged to relate with the author personally, and I can testify that he presented the fruit of his life in this book.

Rev Dr I. O. Mathew's life is evidence of unique grace, and through the gracious words contained herein, I am sure you won't miss the unlimited power of God packaged in these pages.

You will learn how to program circumstances in your favor. What is upon you controls what is around you, but you need a trigger, just like the clearly outlined cases in this book, for example, the widow who was sinking in life-threatening debts but eventually escaped by prophetic programming.

Hence, this book is a prophetic agenda that can break your limits. You will not settle for less where there is more.

This book is from God through man to you for unlimited possibilities.

**Bishop Albert Chikuni**
**General Overseer Family Life Christian Centre,**
**Harare, Zimbabwe.**

# Foreword

It is with great honor and spiritual responsibility that I write this foreword to *Almost Rich: Lessons from the Bible's Richest Woman Who Never Was*, authored by my dear brother and fellow laborer in the vineyard of Christ, Dr. Matthew Omondiale.

This book is not a casual reflection but a Spirit-breathed message for the Body of Christ in our time. Dr. Omondiale, with pastoral insight and prophetic clarity, revisits the account of the widow in 2 Kings 4—a story many know but few have fully understood. In his hands, it becomes more than a record of debt cancellation; it is a Kingdom manual on faith, obedience, and stewardship.

The central truth is striking: this woman stood at the threshold of extraordinary wealth, yet because she underestimated her own oil and did not fully embrace the divine instruction, she settled for less. She became almost rich. Through her story, Dr. Omondiale warns the Church of the danger of partial obedience, misplaced expectation, and the tragic pattern of living beneath the inheritance that God has already secured for His children.

The message of this book is deeply relevant. Many believers today, like that widow, cry out for divine intervention while ignoring the oil already in their house. What they call "nothing" is the very seed God intends to multiply. Dr. Omondiale reminds us that our role is to acknowledge what we have, shut the door to distraction, obey divine instructions completely, and pour out what God has given us. It is in that pouring—whether in ministry, business, or service—that multiplication is released.

What commends this work further is its balance. It is not a book of empty inspiration, nor is it bound by dry theory. It marries the supernatural with the practical, faith with responsibility, vision with action. It dismantles excuses while stirring holy ambition. It is a prophetic call to rise above "almost" and step into the fullness of Kingdom abundance—not merely for personal gain, but for generational impact and the glory of God.

I commend this book to you with full conviction. Read it prayerfully. Receive it not only as instruction but as impartation. I believe that as you engage with these pages, your faith will be quickened, your perspective will be sharpened, and your oil will begin to flow again.

With joy and assurance, I present to you the labor of a faithful servant, Dr. Matthew Omondiale. May Almost Rich be a catalyst for your journey into the richness of life God has prepared for you.

# Introduction

*"⁴ What is man, that thou art mindful of him? and the son of man, that thou visitest him? ⁵ For thou hast made him a little lower than the angels, and hast crowned him with glory and honour. ⁶ Thou madest him to have dominion over the works of thy hands; thou hast put all things under his feet."* **Psalm 8:4-6 (KJV)**

By nature, man is created to be limitless. God has put all things under man. The world is gradually metamorphosing into a new world order, and only those with the right mindset and attitude will stand out. You are powerful. There is no situation that is above you.

*"⁶ And the Lord said, Behold, the people is one, and they have all one language; and this they begin to do: and now nothing will be restrained from them, which they have imagined to do."* **Genesis 11:6 (KJV)**

Man is so powerful that when he thought of erecting a structure that could reach the heavens, God had to act quickly to stop him. The interesting thing in the text is that God acknowledged that nothing could stop man. The only force that is powerful enough to stop you is you.

How much will you invest in a business in which you are guaranteed 100% of profit? How fast will you go if you are sure of your destination? For the purpose of this book, as our case study, we will be looking into the story of a certain widow who had the rare opportunity to change her financial fortune and also make history but missed out on writing her name on the sands of time as the richest woman that ever lived in her days. All she wanted was to pay her debt, but the instruction that carried her solution was capable of making her a global financial icon, and she missed out on that. Whenever you seek God's intervention on a matter, always remember, according to the scriptures, that God does exceedingly and abundantly more than we can ever ask or imagine. Imagine the unbelievable things you think about and wish you could achieve, but in reality, they seem impossible to you. The fact that you can imagine them means that they are achievable. *If God* can do more than you can imagine, what then can you imagine that he cannot do?

> "*58 And he did not many mighty works there because of their unbelief.*" **Matthew 13:58 (KJV)**

We serve a God who is limitless but limited by the limitations we place on him through our unbelief. Faith is not just about positive confession but deep conviction backed up by works. There are so much God wants to do for you and with you but your unbelief displayed through your disobedience and sometimes partial obedience is what has limited him.

> "*20 And Jesus said unto them, Because of your unbelief: for verily I say unto you, If ye have faith as a grain of mustard seed, ye shall say unto this mountain, Remove hence to yonder place; and it shall remove; and nothing shall be impossible unto you.*" **Matthew 17:20 (KJV)**

Nothing is impossible to those who believe.

# Chapter 1

# What Do You Have?

*"1 Now there cried a certain woman of the wives of the sons of the prophets unto Elisha, saying, Thy servant my husband is dead; and thou knowest that thy servant did fear the Lord: and the creditor is come to take unto him my two sons to be bondmen. 2 And Elisha said unto her, what shall I do for thee? tell me, what hast thou in the house? And she said, thine handmaid hath not any thing in the house, save a pot of oil. 3 Then he said, Go, borrow thee vessels abroad of all thy neighbors, even empty vessels; borrow not a few. 4 And when thou art come in, thou shalt shut the door upon thee and upon thy sons, and shalt pour out into all those vessels, and thou shalt set aside that which is full. 5 So she went from him, and shut the door upon her and upon her sons, who brought the vessels to her; and she poured out. 6 And it came to pass, when the vessels were full, that she said unto her son, Bring me yet a vessel. And he said unto her, there is not a vessel more. And the oil stayed. 7 Then she came and told the*

*man of God. And he said, Go, sell the oil, and pay thy debt, and live thou and thy children of the rest."* **2 Kings 4:1-7 (KJV)**

The biggest problem of this generation is that people don't know what they have. This chapter shall focus on solving that problem as you go through the pages with interest.

From our anchor scripture, the widow in the context came to the prophet to ask for financial assistance in order to save her children from being used to pay the debt of their late father, who used them as collateral for a loan he was unable to pay before he died. This woman came expecting the man of God to help her pay her debt but certainly did not expect the kind of response she received from the prophet hence, we see her first response to the question the prophet asked when she initially denied having anything. The first lesson to learn from the widow was not her coming with expectations but how she was expecting. It is good always to have expectations when making a request, but how you expect matters a lot in how you receive it. In particular, when seeking divine intervention, you must always have this in mind: God's ways are not man's ways.

> *"9 For as the heavens are higher than the earth, so are my ways higher than your ways, and my thoughts than your thoughts."* **Isaiah 55:9 (KJV)**

The woman failed to realize that she had something to offer, and perhaps the late husband, too, wouldn't have died a debtor if he had only realized what he had. The issue is not that we don't have anything, but what we lack is the ability to see or acknowledge what we have. **Never say I don't have.** There is nothing God is going to do for you that he is not going to take from you. Your solution is in your problem. All you need to meet your needs is in you. God is never going to do a new thing for you that he hasn't already done for you.

> *"2And on the seventh day God ended his work which he had made; and he rested on the seventh day from all his work which he had made."* **Genesis 2:2 (KJV)**

The above scripture means that God is never going to make anything new ever again because he has rested from all his work. But something interesting happened after God decided to rest: He found out that the man whom he had made needed a companion, and instead of creating another Adam afresh from the earth, he took it from him to make him a companion.

> *"20 And Adam gave names to all cattle, and to the fowl of the air, and to every beast of the field; but for Adam there was not found a help meet for him. 21And the LORD God caused a deep sleep to fall upon Adam, and he slept: and he took one of his ribs, and closed up the flesh instead thereof; 22And the rib, which the LORD God had taken from man, made he a woman, and brought her unto the man. 23 And Adam said, this is now bone of my bones, and flesh of my flesh: she shall be called Woman, because she was taken out of Man."* **Genesis 2:20-23 (KJV)**

Many people know what they want and also know that they need to have something in order to get what they want. But they lack the ability to know what they have in order for them to get what they want. This is not because they don't have it, but they just don't know what they have. This chapter will open your eyes to help you know what you have to get what you want but don't know you have it.

Adam needed a companion, but all he had was a rib, and from it, God made him a woman. What do you have?

## How to know what you have?

The reason why many of us don't know what we have is because we are always looking for what looks like what we want. The seed does not always look like the fruit. We also always undermine what we have because we don't know who we are.

> "*1 And the sons of the prophets said unto Elisha, Behold now, the place where we dwell with thee is too strait for us. 2 Let us go, we pray thee, unto Jordan, and take thence every man a beam, and let us make us a place there, where we may dwell. And he answered, Go ye. 3 And one said, Be content, I pray thee, and go with thy servants. And he answered, I will go. 4 So he went with them. And when they came to Jordan, they cut down wood. 5 But as one was felling a beam, the axe head fell into the water: and he cried, and said, Alas, master! for it was borrowed. 6 And the man of God said, where fell it? And he showed him the place. And he cut down a stick, and cast it in thither; and the iron did swim. 7Therefore said he, Take it up to thee. And he put out his hand and took it.*"
> **2 Kings 6:1-7 (KJV)**

How can a stick cause an axe head to float? Elisha defeated the law of gravity by using what he had to get what he wanted. **All you need is what you have NOW**. When you stop looking for what looks like exactly what you want, then you will find what you have to get what you want.

When what you have cannot get you what you want, place it in God's hand. All the woman needed was the blessing of the man of God on the little bottle of oil.

I learnt this principle a long time ago as a teenager from my Spiritual Father, Archbishop Benson Idahosa, as he shared with us during one of the youth camp meetings in Benin City many years ago. He shared how he founded Christian Faith University, now known as Benson Idahosa University. He had only twenty-one thousand naira left in his account when God told Benson to build him a Christian University, which should be the first in Nigeria to be owned by a Pentecostal church. All he did was lift up his account balance to heaven for God to see, and then he went ahead to lay the foundation and begin to build. Today, that university is known as one of the best outstanding private universities in Nigeria, graduating students who are making global impacts.

My wife can attest to the fact that I have achieved all that I have ever acquired and have done by "faith" in what I have.

Don't you wonder why people mostly want to give to those who already have more than they do to those who don't have? The answer is in the words of Jesus Christ below;

> *"29 For unto everyone that hath shall be given, and he shall have abundance: but from him that hath not shall be taken away even that which he hath."*
> **Matthew 25:29 (KJV)**

This is the same reason why the rich keep getting richer while the poor get poorer. The poor always undermine what they have and keep saying they don't have. It is contradicting to say that *"from he that hath not shall be taken away even that which he hath."* If he had not, then what is it that he has that will now be taken from him? This is to further let us know that no man has nothing. Beloved, you always have something.

Therefore, it is an error for you to say you don't have; you lose what you have the moment you say that.

This same principle is used by all financial institutions. If you have nothing, you get nothing from the banks. You can start making money tomorrow as soon as possible by starting to build your financial records today. I once had a bank account that was dormant for a while because I didn't need it at that time. But I later got into a business deal that required me to use that account more often, and suddenly, I started receiving calls from the bank offering me different packages and even a credit card. You must understand that in the world we live in, no one gives to those who don't have.

> *"15 And the Lord said unto Moses, wherefore criest thou unto me? speak unto the children of Israel, that they go forward:16But lift thou up thy rod, and stretch out thine hand over the sea, and divide it: and the children of Israel shall go on dry ground through the midst of the sea."* **Exodus 14:15-16 (KJV)**

We all have those moments in our lives when we go through difficult situations and need divine intervention or a bail-out. Have you ever found yourself in a position where you have just escaped a challenge, and just when you are about to celebrate, something bigger shows up, making it seem like where you just escaped from is better than where you are now? Moses cried to the Lord, and I will advise you to do the same whenever you are in a position, and you don't know what to do. At that time only God can help you realize what you have in your hands. God wants to use what you have in your hands.

> *"13There hath no temptation taken you but such as is common to man: but God is faithful, who will not suffer you to be tempted above that ye are able; but will with the temptation also make a way to escape, that ye may be able to bear it."*
> **1 Corinthians 10:13 (KJV)**

Your solution is in your problem. God told me this many years ago when I was still struggling to pay the church rent, and from that day, I received my deliverance from worries over the church rentals to making extra money from the church building we were renting. Every problem you face in life comes with a solution.

*"34 And Jesus, when He came out, saw a great multitude and was moved with compassion for them because they were like sheep not having a shepherd. So, He began to teach them many things. 35 When the day was now far spent, His disciples came to Him and said, "This is a deserted place, and already the hour is late. 36Send them away, that they may go into the surrounding country and villages and buy themselves [a]bread; for they have nothing to eat." 37 But He answered and said to them, "You give them something to eat."And they said to Him, "Shall we go and buy two hundred denarii worth of bread and give them something to eat?" 38 But He said to them, "How many loaves do you have? Go and see." And when they found out, they said, "Five, and two fish." 39 Then He commanded them to make them all sit down in groups on the green grass. 40 So they sat down in ranks, in hundreds and in fifties. 41 And when He had taken the five loaves and the two fish, He looked up to heaven, blessed and broke the loaves, and gave them to His disciples to set before them; and the two fish He divided among them all. 42 So they all ate and were filled. 43 And they took up twelve baskets full of fragments and of the fish. 44 Now those who had eaten the loaves were [b]about five thousand men."* **Mark 6:34-44 (NKJV)**

No matter how empty and hungry you are, you must have something that God can bless. His blessing makes one rich. Jesus could have called down man from heaven to feed the people, but he didn't. Instead, he asked for what they had available.

Never give God an empty land; otherwise, you will reap only grass. However, when you give him land with seeds, you reap fruits.

God does not bless your hands but what you have in your hands. It all begins by acknowledging and believing that you have something and what you have doesn't have to be as big as what you want.

Just as the amount of salt needed for a pot of soup to be tasteful does not have to be as large as the size of the pot, that's how you need to understand: what you need to get what you want doesn't have to be as big as what you want. Stop underestimating your potential.

*"20And Jesus said unto them, Because of your unbelief: for verily I say unto you, If ye have faith as a grain of mustard seed, ye shall say unto this mountain, Remove hence to yonder place; and it shall remove; and nothing shall be impossible*

*unto you."* **Matthew 17:20 (KJV)**

What is that mountain confronting you today? Archbishop Benson Idahosa always said if your faith says YES, God will not say NO. Don't wait to develop a "big" faith before you confront it. Jesus said your little faith is all you need.

Before you move to the next chapter of this book, you have to answer these two important questions below:

1. What do I want now?
2. What do I have now to get what I want?

# Chapter 2

# Borrow

*"3Then he said, Go, borrow thee vessels abroad of all thy neighbours, even empty vessels; borrow not a few."* **2 Kings 4:3 (KJV)**

God's blessings often come with specific instructions, and you miss the outcome of the blessing once you miss the instructions. To most people, as in the case of this woman, the blessing is in the instruction. If you cannot follow instructions, then the blessing is not for you. You have to understand that the blessing, in this context, is *the superimposing of divinity on a natural substance to defy natural laws in order to bring about a desired result different from current realities.*

A lot of people fail here and remain slaves to their lender because they don't get any instructions at all or lack the ability to follow divine instructions. From our case study, we realize that the Prophet Elisha was asking the woman to do the exact thing her husband did that plunged her and her two sons into trouble, which was to "go borrow." However, the outcome became different because one was following divine instructions while the other was acting on the flesh.

Being able to differentiate between situations that require borrowing and those that don't depends on your ability to listen and adhere to instructions. Never borrow to solve problems that do not require you to borrow. Some temporary relief measures, such as borrowing, can lead you into a lifetime of slavering and suffering.

When seeking divine intervention, basic things must be put in place:

1. Listen carefully
2. Avoid unnecessary analysis

## Listen Carefully:

*"15He that hath ears to hear, let him hear."*
**Matthew 11:15 (KJV)**

Unfortunately, listening is a skill many in this generation don't have. So many have ears but cannot hear, and those that hear have a partial hearing syndrome, making them miss vital information.

> *"24Then the Lord rained upon Sodom and upon Gomorrah brimstone and fire from the Lord out of heaven; 25And he overthrew those cities, and all the plain, and all the inhabitants of the cities, and that which grew upon the ground. 26 But his wife looked back from behind him, and she became a pillar of salt."* **Genesis 19:24-26 (KJV)**

When following divine instructions, total and complete obedience is required. Your level of listening to instructions is demonstrated in how you follow instructions, not how quiet you are when the instructions are being given. Just a little disobedience in following the instructions given to Lot's wife and family led to her turning into a pillar of salt.

> *"1But a certain man named Ananias, with Sapphira his wife, sold a possession, 2 And kept back part of the price, his wife also being privy to it, and brought a certain part, and laid it at the apostles' feet. 3 But Peter said, Ananias, why hath Satan filled thine heart to lie to the Holy Ghost, and to keep back part of the price of the land? 4Whiles it remained, was it not thine own? and*

*after it was sold, was it not in thine own power? why hast thou conceived this thing in thine heart? thou hast not lied unto men, but unto God. ⁵ And Ananias hearing these words fell down, and gave up the ghost: and great fear came on all them that heard these things. ⁶ And the young men arose, wound him up, and carried him out, and buried him. ⁷ And it was about the space of three hours after, when his wife, not knowing what was done, came in. ⁸ And Peter answered unto her, Tell me whether ye sold the land for so much? And she said, Yea, for so much. ⁹ Then Peter said unto her, how is it that ye have agreed together to tempt the Spirit of the Lord? behold, the feet of them which have buried thy husband are at the door and shall carry thee out. ¹⁰ Then fell she down straightway at his feet and yielded up the ghost: and the young men came in, and found her dead, and, carrying her forth, buried her by her husband. ¹¹ And great fear came upon all the church, and upon as many as heard these things."*
**Acts 5:1-11 (KJV)**

Partial obedience carries dire consequences, just as not obeying at all. I believe that Ananias and their wife weren't the only ones with lands, nor were they the only ones who brought their proceeds from the sales of their lands to give to God. Nothing would have happened to them if they hadn't sold the land nor given anything, but because it was a willful offering and it was their decision to give, they had to give the right way as instructed, and their failure to do so led to their untimely death. In our days, you may not die physically, but something dies in you whenever you fail to heed to divine instructions or decide to obey partially.

> *"10 And Elisha sent a messenger unto him, saying, Go and wash in Jordan seven times, and thy flesh shall come again to thee, and thou shalt be clean."*
> **2 Kings 5:10 (KJV)**

> *"14 Then went he down, and dipped himself seven times in Jordan, according to the saying of the man of God: and his flesh came again like unto the flesh of a little child, and he was clean."*
> **2 Kings 5:14 (KJV)**

God does not reward partial obedience. It was recorded that Naaman only got his miracle when he came out of the water the seventh time. If he had only done it six times and left the water, he would have still remained with his leprosy, and all his efforts would have gone to waste. *Stop demonstrating partial obedience and expecting full results.*

I must, however, not fail to note here that you must not allow your desperation to push you to take the voice of greedy, self-acclaimed men of God as the voice of God, lest you fall prey to their manipulation. It is your responsibility to design the voice of God from the voice of men.

## Avoid Unnecessary Analysis

Too much of analysis leads to paralysis. Divine instructions do not always make sense to natural men. Most people don't receive the fulfillment of their prophecies because they analyze spiritual things through their canal senses or experiences.

*"10 And Elisha sent a messenger unto him, saying, Go and wash in Jordan seven times, and thy flesh shall come again to thee, and thou shalt be clean.*

*11 But Naaman was wroth, and went away, and said, Behold, I thought, He will surely come out to me, and stand, and call on the name of the Lord his God, and strike his hand over the place, and recover the leper. 12 Are not Abana and Pharpar, rivers of Damascus, better than all the waters of*

*Israel? may I not wash in them, and be clean? So he turned and went away in a rage. 13 And his servants came near, and spake unto him, and said, my father, if the prophet had bid thee do some great thing, wouldest thou not have done it? how much rather then, when he saith to thee, Wash, and be clean? 14Then went he down, and dipped himself seven times in Jordan, according to the saying of the man of God: and his flesh came again like unto the flesh of a little child, and he was clean."* **2 Kings 5:10-14 (KJV)**

For as long as Naaman continued to analyze what the man of God instructed him to do, his situation remained the same. Your compliance with divine instruction is what brings about the desired results.

## How and Where to Borrow

Borrowing is a good way to get your debt paid, bail yourself out of hard times, make progress in certain situations, actualize your dreams, and live a better life, but only if we know how to borrow and where to borrow from in times of need. The prophet told the lady to go borrow from all her neighbors and not to borrow a few. We shall be explaining that later, but first, let's see how and where you can borrow, most especially "money."

## DISCLAIMER:

> I am not a certified financial expert, and whatever I'm about to share below is from personal experiences and research and, thus, my personal opinion and counsel.

## Special Note:

You've got choices if you want to borrow money: whether you need to finance emergency expenses, make home improvements, or actualize a dream. Looking at just one option could cost you a lot, so be sure to examine all the alternatives to help you make the smartest money move for you.

Fortunately, there are a number of borrowing options. Aside from a traditional bank, some borrowing options include a credit union, online lender, payday or car-title lender, pawn shop, credit card, a friend or family member, and a 401(k) retirement account.

But not all of these options are for everyone. For

example, you might not own valuables to pawn, or you might not have a 401(k), which is mainly available in the United States of America.

Plus, each of these eight options has its own advantages and disadvantages. Let's delve into what to consider before you decide where or if to borrow money.

## 1. Banks:

Taking out a personal loan from a bank can seem like an attractive option. For example, some banks offer perks like no loan initiation fee, which often ranges from 1% to 8%. This loan initiation fee usually covers the lender's administrative expenses for processing your application and paying you the money.

You also may qualify for an interest-rate discount — sometimes referred to as a relationship discount — if you're an existing customer at a bank that offers this perk. They offer loyalty discounts on the interest rate if you maintain qualifying bank accounts and enroll in automatic payments.

But keep in mind that some big banks don't offer personal loans. While some banks may require you to have good or excellent credit to get approval for a personal loan, others, mostly in Africa, will require you to have collateral equivalent to the market value of what you may be asking for.

## 2. Credit Unions

A personal loan from a credit union might be a better option than a personal loan from a bank. Why?

For one thing, a credit union may offer lower interest rates and fees than a bank. Since credit unions are not-for-profits dedicated to serving members, their goal is to return profit to members instead of shareholders.

However, you must meet a credit union's membership eligibility requirements in order to become a member. This can include residence in a certain country, a connection to a specific school or employer, or family ties to a current member.

## 3. Online Lenders

In the digital age, online lenders have sprung up as an alternative to traditional personal loans from banks and credit unions.

Online lenders aren't tied down by the costs that come with maintaining physical branches. And they often offer the user experience that people have come to expect from digital loan applications. An efficient funding process and easy-to-navigate online applications are crucial for customer satisfaction, according to a press release by J.D. Power.

Many online lenders promise fast funding, with money deposited into your bank account as soon as one or two business days if you're approved.

But if it's not a lender you're familiar with, research its reputation online and check with traditional lenders to see if they can offer better interest rates and terms.

## 4. Payday lenders

A payday loan is typically a short-term loan for an amount that's usually little. You can apply for payday loans online or at a payday loan storefront near you. Keep in mind that payday loans are an expensive form of financing, and if possible, consider other funding options.

A payday loan typically must be repaid by your next payday. Terms and rates vary by state, but a payday lender usually charges a percentage or dollar amount for each $100 borrowed. The Consumer Financial Protection Bureau says a common scenario is a fee of $15 per $100 — that works out to an annual percentage rate of nearly 400% for a two-week loan.

If a borrower is unable to pay the loan and the fees, the lender might be permitted to extend the due date, adding even more fees to the original amount owed. This type of loan is only available in certain countries.

## 5. Pawn shops

A pawn shop loan differs from a traditional personal loan in a critical way: A pawn loan involves no credit check or application process. The amount of money you borrow from a pawnshop is based on the value of the item you're pawning. According to the

National Pawnbrokers Association, the average pawn shop loan in the U.S. is $150.

While a pawn shop loan can be a quick source of cash when you need money, this form of borrowing can be problematic. Interest rates are often high — commonly ranging from 5% to 25% — and various fees might be tacked on. And if you fail to pay off the loan when you're supposed to, the pawn shop can sell the item you pawned. Consider all your options before proceeding with this kind of loan.

## 6. Cash advance from credit card

Using a credit card to access cash can seem like an appealing option. Since you already have the card, you don't have to fill out an application or go through a credit check to get what essentially is a short-term loan against the line of credit available on your credit card. Plus, you can typically access the money quickly.

However, the simplicity of a credit card cash advance can come at a price. Some card issuers charge a fee to get a cash advance along with an interest rate that's usually high. Also, most credit cards don't provide a grace period for cash advances, meaning that the interest charges start the moment you withdraw the cash.

## 7. Family and friends

Getting a loan from a family member or friend may seem like an uncomplicated way to get cash when you need it. After all, a family loan might come with no contract — or a basic contract, and you might get a very favorable interest rate even without excellent credit.

But things can get complicated if a dispute arises over repayment of the loan. What if you still owe $5,000 to Uncle Michael? That can cause a lot of awkwardness. Another thing to think about is since your friend or relative can't report your loan payments to the three major credit bureaus, you won't reap any credit-building benefits.

## 8. 401(k) retirement account

Borrowing money from your employer-sponsored 401(k) requires no credit check. And if your 401(k) plan allows loans, you can borrow $10,000 or 50% of your vested account balance, whichever is greater, though the cap on 401(k) loans is $50,000.

You must repay the 401(k) loan within five years, and the interest you pay on the loan goes back into your 401(k).

Although accessing cash from your 401(k) sounds simple, consider some of the consequences. For instance, leaving your job could force you to repay the loan in full before your next federal tax return is due. If you can't repay the loan, you might be hit with tax penalties.

And don't forget you'll be missing out on investment returns on money you pull out of your 401(k).

Please note that some of the above-listed mediums you can borrow may not be available to all as they vary from country to country.

## Note:

The above on where to borrow money was written by John Egan and partly edited for the purpose of this publication. Some of the prescribed loan avenues may not be available in some countries. The use of dollars is for illustration purposes as it is primarily predominant in the global market.

## Bottom line

Whether you need fast cash or a long-term loan, you should take the time to research loan options and ask questions before you borrow money. Here are some key questions to think about.

- Why do I need the money, and which type of loan best fits that need?
- What is the interest rate?
- Are there any fees associated with the loan?
- How long do I have to pay back the loan?
- What happens if I can't pay back the loan?
- Will a creditor perform a hard credit check that will affect my credit reports?

## How You Should Not Borrow

- Never borrow for fun
- Never borrow to please anyone
- Never borrow to show off
- Never borrow to spend
- Never borrow to satisfy your ego
- Never borrow to satisfy an addiction

*"3 Then he said, Go, borrow thee vessels abroad of all thy neighbors, even empty vessels; borrow not a few. 4 And when thou art come in, thou shalt shut the door upon thee and upon thy sons, and shalt pour out into all those vessels, and thou shalt set aside that which is full. 5 So she went from him, and shut the door upon her and upon her sons, who brought the vessels to her; and she poured out. 6 And it came to pass, when the vessels were full, that she said unto her son, Bring me yet a vessel. And he said unto her, there is not a vessel more. And the oil stayed."* **2 Kings 4:3-6 (KJV)**

In our case, one of the biggest mistakes made by the widow in the text is that she did not borrow well. It may seem like she got what she wanted, but our focus for this book is on the instructions she received and what she could have achieved if she had followed them correctly. The fact that she could ask her children for more vessels showed her nonchalant attitude towards the instructions she received. She didn't make an effort to go borrow as instructed but sent her children instead. She defied the instructions of her major lifetime breakthrough. Take note of the highlighted words in the text below:

*"³ Then he said, **Go, borrow** thee vessels **abroad** of all thy neighbors, even empty vessels; **borrow not a few**."*

The above-highlighted words were enough to make the woman *"The richest woman"* in history, but she failed just by undermining a prophetic instruction. Many of us are living below the average of God's original plan for us because of our lack of ability to recognize life-changing divine instructions. But by the mercies of God, I declare: may your eyes and ears be open henceforth to hear and see life-changing opportunities wrapped in divine instructions in Jesus Christ's name. Amen.

# Chapter 3

# Shut Your Door

*"⁴And when thou art come in, thou shalt shut the door upon thee and upon thy sons, and shalt pour out into all those vessels, and thou shalt set aside that which is full."*

### 2 Kings 4:4 King James Version (KJV)

A door is a hinged or otherwise movable barrier that allows ingress and egress into an "enclosure". It is mainly for the purpose of securing an area. A door can also be seen as a movable structure used for opening and closing an entrance or for giving access to something. Simply put, a door is meant to give access or deny access to an area or place.

*There are certain things that have to be kept behind closed doors until an appointed time before revealing them.* Every sensible carpenter has a workshop separate from his showroom. Items in the workshop are kept away from the eyes of potential clients until they are ready for the showroom. Many projects have been aborted because they were exposed prematurely. I was told the original owner of the *selfie stick* idea posted a sample of it on YouTube a week into its mass production, and before the end of that week, some Chinese guys had stolen the concept and flooded the market with the same stick at a cheaper price. There are people you must never share your idea with; they must only see the end result of your work.

> "*10And Joshua had commanded the people, saying, Ye shall not shout, nor make any noise with your voice, neither shall any word proceed out of your mouth, until the day I bid you shout; then shall ye shout.*"
>
> **Joshua 6:10 King James Version (KJV)**

There are days you just have to walk in silence and ignore whatever the enemy might be saying. I can imagine how much the people of Jericho could be mocking the Israelites, seeing them walk around their walls aimlessly and helplessly, but for several days, according to divine instructions, they walked around the walls in silence. There are times you just have to keep your explanation to yourself and let your work speak for itself. Whatever the Lord told Joshua to instruct the Israelites at this time was not the most logical thing to do, considering the situation that they were confronted with. A man under divine instruction has nothing to explain to the natural mind, whose opinion is only tied to logic and human senses, because they will never understand, no matter how you try to explain. No man can successfully follow God and listen to men at the same time.

The moment the woman opened the door to go borrow more vessels, the oil stopped running. *The anointing is released in the secret place but demonstrated in the public place.* Any man of God you see demonstrating the power of God did not get it on the pulpit but behind the pulpit. Behind closed doors is where life is conceived and born, destinies commissioned and released. Stop seeking public opinion over certain issues in your life. Shut your door, have a meeting with yourself and begin to let that oil within you flow. For in you lies a stream of living waters.

> *"16 And it came to pass, when she pressed him daily with her words, and urged him, so that his soul was vexed unto death; 17 That he told her all his heart, and said unto her, There hath not come a razor upon mine head; for I have been a Nazarite unto God from my mother's womb: if I be shaven, then my strength will go from me, and I shall become weak, and be like any other man. 18 And when Delilah saw that he had told her all his heart, she sent and called for the lords of the Philistines, saying, come up this once, for he hath shewed me all his heart. Then the lords of the Philistines came up unto her, and brought money in their hand."*

**Judges 16:16-18 King James Version (KJV)**

Most of the time, we mistake those who are with us for those who are for us. The fact that somebody is with you does not mean that they are for you. Some may just be spies in your camp. You need to have the spirit of discernment to be able to differentiate those who are with you from those who are for you. This is because most of the time those that are with you are often smooth talkers, eye service and busy bodies and can appear to be more loyal and sometimes sacrificial than everyone else.

Learn to make progress in silence and let people continue to wonder about the secret of your success. There are certain secrets that must be known to you alone. Samson serves as a lesson to all those romancing with a friendly enemy. A friendly enemy is not your friend but still an enemy. Never mistake their friendliness for friendship and loyalty.

> *"13And Hezekiah hearkened unto them, and shewed them all the house of his precious things, the silver, and the gold, and the spices, and the precious ointment, and all the house of his armour, and all that was found in his treasures: there was nothing in his house, nor in all his dominion, that Hezekiah shewed them not.* *14 Then came Isaiah the prophet unto king Hezekiah, and said unto him, what said these men? and from whence came they unto thee? And Hezekiah said, they are come from a far country, even from Babylon. 15 And he said, what have they seen in thine house? And Hezekiah answered, All the things that are in mine house have they seen: there is nothing among my treasures that I have not shewed them. 16 And Isaiah said unto*

*Hezekiah, Hear the word of the Lord. [17] Behold, the days come, that all that is in thine house, and that which thy fathers have laid up in store unto this day, shall be carried into Babylon: nothing shall be left, saith the Lord."*

**2 Kings 20:13-17 King James Version**

No matter how liberal you are, there are things and places in your home that must be restricted to strangers. A man lost a generational inheritance that was passed on to him and subsequently was supposed to pass on to his children. But because he let strangers into the secret of his family's wealth, he lost it all. Learn to protect your secret place by shutting your door to strangers. Many have lost fortunes that they should be passing on to their offspring and generations after them, just by revealing sensitive information about their business to strangers. *Learn to shut your workshop to people who have nothing to contribute to the work.* Stop allowing visitors and friends to enter during your working hours. The prophet told the lady to shut her door while she was busy pouring her oil. Work and pleasure do not mix. There is a reason why your house is divided into sections with doors to give you access to different sections. It's not just for decoration or beautification but for restriction purposes. There's no use for a beautiful, tall gate without a lock. I weep for the children of King Hezekiah who had to suffer greatly for the carelessness of their father. Before you open that door to strangers, remember King Hezekiah's innocent children who were born as princes with royal blood but died as slaves in another man's palace, decorated with their inheritance just because their father failed to shut his doors.

*"20 Go home, my people, and lock your doors! Hide yourselves for a little while until the Lord's anger has passed"*

**Isaiah 26:20 New Living Translation**

There are times you must learn to isolate yourself behind closed doors to enable yourself to refresh. Take time to periodically scan through the system of your heart using the antivirus of your conscience. Switch off from all forms of communications with others, press the reboot button and refresh the applications of your mind. Uninstall, reinstall and refresh your system before you open your doors again.

*"⁵When you pray, don't be like the hypocrites who love to pray publicly on street corners and in the synagogues where everyone can see them. I tell you the truth, that is all the reward they will ever get. ⁶ But when you pray, go away by yourself, shut the door behind you, and pray to your Father in private. Then your Father, who sees everything, will reward you."*

**Matthew 6:5-6 New Living Translation**

The secret behind the success of Christ's ministry on earth was greatly tied to his unexplainable disappearance from people from time to time, isolating himself in a secret place to communicate with his father. *If you do not develop the habit of shutting yourself in, you will soon be shut out from the global space of relevance.* Every athlete who is relevant in our day trains more hours than they play in a real match. Jesus admonishes us in the scriptures to develop the habit of praying behind closed doors.

*"²⁰ And when he had taken him, and brought him to his mother, he sat on her knees till noon, and then died. ²¹ And she went up, and laid him on the bed of the man of God, and shut the door upon him, and went out."*

<br>

*Dr. Matthew Omondiale*

## 2 Kings 4:20-21 King James Version

Most problems get complicated when we relate them to certain people, especially those who have no solution to the problems. This woman had a choice, like every other woman to cry and gather neighbors to sympathize with her over her situation, but she chose to shut her problem behind her in search of her solution. Stop gathering people over an issue that requires you to shut your door.

*"32 And when Elisha came into the house, behold, the child was dead, and laid upon his bed. 33 He went in therefore, and shut the door upon them twain, and prayed unto the Lord. 34 And he went up, and lay upon the child, and put his mouth upon his mouth, and his eyes upon his eyes, and his hands upon his hands: and stretched himself upon the child; and the flesh of the child waxed warm. 35 Then he returned, and walked in the house to and fro; and went up, and stretched himself upon him: and the child sneezed seven times, and the child opened his eyes. 36 And he called Gehazi, and said, Call this Shunammite. So he called her. And when she was come in unto him, he said, Take up thy son. 37 Then she went in, and fell at his feet, and bowed herself to the ground,*

*and took up her son, and went out."*

**2 Kings 4:32-37 King James Version**

I am challenged by the great faith of this woman. She only went away after she got her miracle. How long are you ready to stay indoors until you get answers? So many are in too much of a hurry and are not willing to wait. There is power in waiting behind closed doors. If you can shut the door with just the Lord and your situation, no matter how dead it may seem, you are sure to go out with a testimony. Someone confronted me for not letting him know my wife was pregnant. My simple question to him was, "Did you get my wife pregnant?" That was the end of that conversation. Stop entertaining casual talks that may lead you to revealing sensitive information. Pregnancy is not something you announce; it's what people should see in due time because no one can cover a pregnancy with their hands for nine months. There is a reason the womb of a pregnant woman does not shoot out in the first few weeks of pregnancy. Miscarriage is easier to occur in the early stages, and that's why God keeps the formative days away from public eyes: so, the wicked does not see it.

There are business ideas and other opportunities you must treat like pregnancy.

Allow people to see for themselves when it's mature enough. There is no need to announce to the neighborhood that you are going to the garage to buy a car when you are actually going to drive the car home. A car is not something you can hide in your wardrobe for people not to see; it's something that reveals itself. Stop revealing what is meant to reveal itself; most times, we abort our fortunes by exposing them prematurely to others. Not all eyes are witnesses; some are monitoring spirits. The beauty of every door is in its lock; use it. The reason why you keep experiencing those heartbreaks is that you don't know how to use the locks on your doors. The locks are not for decoration but for regulations and restrictive measures. Whether you are praying, working, going through a challenge, starting a business, or about to make a new move, "SHUT YOUR DOOR", period.

# Chapter 4

# Pour Out Your Oil

*"4 And when thou art come in, thou shalt shut the door upon thee and upon thy sons, and shalt pour out into all those vessels, and thou shalt set aside that which is full. 5 So she went from him, and shut the door upon her and upon her sons, who brought the vessels to her; and she poured out. 6 And it came to pass, when the vessels were full, that she said unto her son, Bring me yet a vessel. And he said unto her, there is not a vessel more. And the oil stayed."*

**2 Kings 4:4-6 (King James Version)**

Every oil in a bottle has an expiry date. When oil stays too long in a bottle, it sleeps, and when it stays longer, it loses its value. The purpose of having oil in containers is to distribute it in measures and not to keep it. Oil is meant to flow. The husband of this woman who died had that same oil in the house but was storing it instead of pouring it. What is that oil you are storing?

The efficacy of your oil is in its pouring, not in its storing, irrespective of how beautiful the storage might be. The oil of the woman began to multiply when she began to pour it. There is money you are saving in the bank right now that you should be pouring into some investment that can empower your community, and until you start pouring it, never expect your needs to be met. Money in the bank does not multiply; some even incur charges. I have discovered that poor men save more than the rich. As a matter of fact, poor men take their money to the bank to save, while rich men go to the bank to borrow the money the poor have saved to invest in something to render services to the poor. They then take directly from the poor (through the services they offer) to pay the bank the money the poor saved with them, which they borrowed. Rich men take from the bank more than they save in the bank, while poor men give to the bank more than the bank can give them. I am not against savings, but I am against savings without a purpose. Anything can come to take the money away. The reason God increases you is not to have abundance in your bank account while people around you are lacking basic services.

> *"25 And Joseph said unto Pharaoh, The dream of Pharaoh is one: God hath shewed Pharaoh what he is about to do. 26 The seven good kine are seven years; and the seven good ears are seven years: the dream is one. 27 And the seven thin and ill-favored kine that came up after them are seven years; and the seven empty ears blasted with the east wind shall be seven years of famine. 28 This is the thing which I have spoken unto Pharaoh: What God is about to do he sheweth unto Pharaoh. 29 Behold, there come seven years of great plenty throughout all the land of Egypt: 30 And there shall arise after them seven years of famine; and all the plenty shall be forgotten in the land of Egypt; and the famine shall consume the land; 31 And the plenty shall not be known in the land by reason of that famine following; for it shall be very grievous. 32 And for that the dream was doubled unto Pharaoh twice; it is because the thing is established by God, and God will shortly bring it to pass. 33 Now therefore let Pharaoh look out a man discreet and wise, and set him over the land of Egypt. 34 Let Pharaoh do this, and let him appoint officers over the land, and take up the fifth part of the land of Egypt in the seven plenteous years. 35 And let them gather all the food of those good years that come, and lay up*

*corn under the hand of Pharaoh, and let them keep food in the cities. 36 And that food shall be for store to the land against the seven years of famine, which shall be in the land of Egypt; that the land perish not through the famine. 37 And the thing was good in the eyes of Pharaoh, and in the eyes of all his servants. 38 And Pharaoh said unto his servants, Can we find such a one as this is, a man in whom the Spirit of God is? 39 And Pharaoh said unto Joseph, Forasmuch as God hath shewed thee all this, there is none so discreet and wise as thou art: 40 Thou shalt be over my house, and according unto thy word shall all my people be ruled: only in the throne will I be greater than thou."*

## Genesis 41:25-40 King James Version (KJV)

From the above text, we can see Joseph's counsel to Pharaoh, which eventually led to his elevation in Egypt, that if you must save, it must be for a reason, and it must not also be for the wrong reasons. The Egyptians poured into their banks for the sole purpose of distribution during the period of famine, and as they distributed, they also had more than enough to accommodate people from other countries.

*"16 And he spake a parable unto them, saying, the*

*ground of a certain rich man brought forth plentifully: ¹⁷ And he thought within himself, saying, what shall I do, because I have no room where to bestow my fruits? ¹⁸ And he said, this will I do: I will pull down my barns and build greater; and there will I bestow all my fruits and my goods. ¹⁹ And I will say to my soul, Soul, thou hast much goods laid up for many years; take thine ease, eat, drink, and be merry. ²⁰ But God said unto him, Thou fool, this night thy soul shall be required of thee: then whose shall those things be, which thou hast provided? ²¹ So is he that layeth up treasure for himself, and is not rich toward God."*

## Luke 12:16-21 King James Version (KJV)

Some people are just keeping money in their bank accounts so they can boast about their bank balance to others. The reason you are blessed is to bless others. Archbishop Benson Idahosa once said, *"You are not a millionaire until your millions have touched one million people"*. This means how rich you are is not a function of how much you have but how much you have poured into others. No one has ever become poor by giving to others. God did not take the man's life just because he wanted to save, but because he did not think to acknowledge God as the giver and also to give of his excess harvest to others.

> "36 Now there was at Joppa a certain disciple named Tabitha, which by interpretation is called Dorcas: this woman was full of good works and almsdeeds which she did. 37 And it came to pass in those days, that she was sick, and died: whom when they had washed, they laid her in an upper chamber. 28 And forasmuch as Lydda was nigh to Joppa, and the disciples had heard that Peter was there, they sent unto him two men, desiring him that he would not delay to come to them. 39 Then Peter arose and went with them. When he came, they brought him into the upper chamber: and all the widows stood by him weeping, and shewing the coats and garments which Dorcas made, while she was with them. 40 But Peter put them all forth, and kneeled down, and prayed; and turning him to the body said, Tabitha, arise. And she opened her eyes: and when she saw Peter, she sat up. 41 And he gave her his hand, and lifted her up, and when he had called the saints and widows, presented her alive."

## Acts 9:36-41 King James Version (KJV)

This community of Christians refused to bury this woman (Dorcas) because of the way she poured into the community. What are you pouring into people in your community? Can your community stand to defend you in the days of trouble? Take time out to answer the above questions. Peter was called into the room where the lifeless woman was lying on the bed, but he came out bringing her back to her community alive. You can start pouring today by speaking to someone in your neighborhood about the love of God demonstrated through Jesus Christ, and by sharing some material things with them according to the measure God has blessed you. There are so many empty vessels around us, God is expecting us to pour into them from our oil.

*"1Now Jephthah the Gileadite was a mighty man of valour, and he was the son of a harlot: and Gilead begat Jephthah. 2 And Gilead's wife bare him sons; and his wife's sons grew up, and they thrust out Jephthah, and said unto him, Thou shalt not inherit in our father's house; for thou art the son of a strange woman. 3 Then Jephthah fled from his brethren, and dwelt in the land of Tob: and there were gathered vain men to Jephthah, and went out with him. 4 And it came to pass in process of time, that the children of Ammon made war against Israel. 5 And it was so, that when the children of Ammon made war against Israel, the*

*elders of Gilead went to fetch Jephthah out of the land of Tob: 6 And they said unto Jephthah, Come, and be our captain, that we may fight with the children of Ammon. 7 And Jephthah said unto the elders of Gilead, did not ye hate me, and expel me out of my father's house? and why are ye come unto me now when ye are in distress? 8 And the elders of Gilead said unto Jephthah, Therefore we turn again to thee now, that thou mayest go with us, and fight against the children of Ammon, and be our head over all the inhabitants of Gilead. 9 And Jephthah said unto the elders of Gilead, if ye bring me home again to fight against the children of Ammon, and the Lord deliver them before me, shall I be your head? 10 And the elders of Gilead said unto Jephthah, The Lord be witness between us, if we do not so according to thy words. 11 Then Jephthah went with the elders of Gilead, and the people made him head and captain over them: and Jephthah uttered all his words before the Lord in Mizpeh."*

## Judges 11:1-11 King James Version (KJV)

Jephthah was a great man who poured out his oil to support his father in building the family business. But due to the circumstances surrounding his birth, he was chased out of his inheritance. But the scriptures record that he never gave up, nor did he stop pouring his oil. But this time, in vain, futile, frustrated, ineffective, delusive, fruitless men and with time, he raised a great army out of the same men. After some time, the elders of the entire community where the family of Jephthah, who threw him out, belonged, cried to Jephthah for help when they were under attack, and he didn't hesitate to help them. He eventually became the ruler of the entire community. *Children chased him out as a son, but the elders brought him back as a king.* Don't be discouraged by betrayers and backstabbers. Sometimes, their attitude towards you is part of the plan to ensuring your next level or enthronement. Twenty years after Archbishop Benson Idahosa passed to glory, Pastor Chris Oyakhilome whose ministry had not come into lime light then came back to donate one billion naira to Benson Idahosa University the highest known amount any single religious leader has ever donated to another organization in Nigeria just because of the oil the Archbishop poured on him while he was still alive. Men are vessels. I encourage you today to continue to pour; one day, one of those vessels will pay your bills and meet your needs.

The scripture records that all the vessels in the room were filled as the woman poured. The multiplication ability God gave to man at creation is enforced at this point of pouring.

*"7 And it came to pass after a while, that the brook dried up, because there had been no rain in the land. 8 And the word of the Lord came unto him, saying, 9 Arise, get thee to Zarephath, which belongeth to Zidon, and dwell there: behold, I have commanded a widow woman there to sustain thee. 10 So he arose and went to Zarephath. And when he came to the gate of the city, behold, the widow woman was there gathering of sticks: and he called to her, and said, fetch me, I pray thee, a little water in a vessel, that I may drink. 11 And as she was going to fetch it, he called to her, and said, bring me, I pray thee, a morsel of bread in thine hand. 12 And she said, As the Lord thy God liveth, I have not a cake, but an handful of meal in a barrel, and a little oil in a cruse: and, behold, I am gathering two sticks, that I may go in and dress it for me and my son, that we may eat it, and die. 13 And Elijah said unto her, Fear not; go and do as thou hast said: but make me thereof a little cake first, and bring it unto me,*

*and after making for thee and for thy son. 14 For thus saith the Lord God of Israel, The barrel of meal shall not waste, neither shall the cruse of oil fail, until the day that the Lord sendeth rain upon the earth. 15 And she went and did according to the saying of Elijah: and she, and he, and her house, did eat many days. 16 And the barrel of meal wasted not, neither did the cruse of oil fail, according to the word of the Lord, which he spake by Elijah."*

## 1 Kings 17:7-16 King James Version (KJV)

Bishop Oyedepo once shared his encounter with Archbishop Benson Idahosa. During the early days of his ministry, he was short of some money to pay his workers and he decided to call the Archbishop for help and the Archbishop instructed him to bring what he had and upon getting to his office with what he had, with the hope of getting more to add, the Archbishop instructed him to drop the money and go back to his station. Even though that threw him into deeper confusion, he obeyed and dropped the money, and according to his testimony, the moment he got back to base, one of his followers called him and said he was traveling from Kanu and passing through Kaduna briefly and would love to see him, and he obliged. When the fellow came, he dropped a parcel and left, and when they opened the parcel, it was the exact amount needed to pay the workers. In the words of the archbishop to bishop Oyedepo, he said, "If what you have is not enough to get what you want, then what you have is a seed you need to pour on the ground". In other words, what you have is always enough as a seed if it's not enough to meet your needs. The God who worked with Elijah is still very much at work in our days to those who have enough faith to pour their oil. The food and oil of the widow didn't run dry because she poured them out to honor a prophet. I dare you today to look around you and begin to pour your oil. Pour into that investment, pour into that person, pour into that ministry, pour into that community, pour into that work, pour into that business, pour into that family. Anything and anyone can be the vessels you need to pour into. JUST POUR.

# Chapter 5

# Sell Your Vessels Of Oil

*"7 Then she came and told the man of God. And he said, Go, sell the oil, and pay thy debt, and live thou and thy children of the rest."*

**2 Kings 4:7 King James Version (KJV)**

This is the point where you move your already filled vessels from the workshop to the showroom. Here, you require some marketing techniques in order to sell your product. Unfortunately, many believers fail here because they lack the required skills in this area. This is often as a result of ignorance, religious indoctrinations or affiliations, pride, illiteracy, and many other factors. No matter how much anointing (oil) you carry, and how much it's well packaged, if you lack good marketing skills, no one will buy your product. Some religious Christians believe they should have nothing to do with people of other religions. There's a song that we used to sing growing up in children's Sunday school with tears in our eyes from the book of Psalms.

> *"¹By the rivers of Babylon, there we sat down, yea, we wept, when we remembered Zion. ² We hanged our harps upon the willows in the midst thereof. ³ For there they that carried us away captive required of us a song; and they that wasted us required of us mirth, saying, Sing us one of the songs of Zion. ⁴ How shall we sing the Lord's song in a strange land?"*

**Psalm 137:1-4 King James Version (KJV)**

Now I have come to realize that the children of Israel may have had a good reason not to sing the Lord's song in a strange land then, but we do not have any reason because we were once the strange land they referred to. But Grace was extended to us, and we have been mandated to extend the same to all nations and people of the earth without any form of discrimination or segregation.

> *"⁹ Here's the lesson: Use your worldly resources to benefit others and make friends. Then, when your possessions are gone, they will welcome you to an*

*eternal home.[a]"*

## Luke 16:9 New Living Translation (NLT)

Jesus says, "Make friends." *Maintaining a good relationship makes your product acceptable.* If they don't accept you, they cannot accept your product. One of the greatest battles Jesus had to fight in his ministry was the battle for acceptance.

> *"[52] And Jesus increased in wisdom and stature, and in favour with God and man."*

## Luke 2:52 King James Version (KJV)

Favour from God was not enough for Jesus to do his ministry on earth; he needed favor from men as well. Man is an important factor if you must succeed on earth. You must never make the mistake of choosing money above men.

> *"[2] Now when John had heard in the prison the works of Christ, he sent two of his disciples, [3] And said unto him, Art thou he that should come, or do we look for another?"*

## Matthew 11:2-3 King James Version (KJV)

Imagine being doubted by your forerunner. Who

will believe you? This was the reason Jesus could not perform many miracles in his own city because they did not accept him, and John the Baptist was the major cause because he failed to market Jesus properly to the people as he ought to. Men are ladders we must climb in life in order to fulfill destiny. God does nothing on earth without the instrumentality of a man. You must know how to utilize the services of marketers.

> *"⁴ Now when he had left speaking, he said unto Simon, Launch out into the deep, and let down your nets for a draught. ⁵ And Simon answering said unto him, Master, we have toiled all the night, and have taken nothing: nevertheless at thy word I will let down the net. ⁶ And when they had this done, they inclosed a great multitude of fishes: and their net brake. ⁷ And they beckoned unto their partners, which were in the other ship, that they should come and help them. And they came, and filled both the ships, so that they began to sink."*

> **Luke 5:4-7 (KJV)**

Dr. Charles Awuzie, in one of his posts on Facebook explaining the above scripture, opened my eyes to see this particular verse in a different light: "AND THEY

BECKONED UNTO THEIR OTHER PARTNERS, WHICH WERE IN THE OTHER SHIP." Sometimes we must extend our partnership beyond those within our ship to those in the "other ship". Build partnerships across borders, go beyond your religious, political and ethnic circle and build bridges. David in the scriptures helped King Saul to defeat the Philistine (Goliath), but it was another Philistine (Achish, the king of Gath) who took David into safety when the same King Saul was after his life.

> *"1 Now Naaman, captain of the host of the king of Syria, was a great man with his master, and honorable, because by him the Lord had given deliverance unto Syria: he was also a mighty man in valor, but he was a leper. 2 And the Syrians had gone out by companies, and had brought away captive out of the land of Israel a little maid; and she waited on Naaman's wife. 3 And she said unto her mistress, Would God my lord was with the prophet that is in Samaria! for he would recover him of his leprosy. 4 And one went in, and told his lord, saying, Thus and thus said the maid that is of the land of Israel. 5 And the king of Syria said, Go to, go, and I will send a letter unto the king of Israel. And he departed, and took with him ten*

*talents of silver, and six thousand pieces of gold, and ten changes of raiment. ⁶ And he brought the letter to the king of Israel, saying, Now when this letter is come unto thee, behold, I have therewith sent Naaman my servant to thee, that thou mayest recover him of his leprosy. ⁷ And it came to pass, when the king of Israel had read the letter, that he rent his clothes, and said, Am I God, to kill and to make alive, that this man doth send unto me to recover a man of his leprosy? wherefore consider, I pray you, and see how he seeketh a quarrel against me. ⁸ And it was so, when Elisha the man of God had heard that the king of Israel had rent his clothes, that he sent to the king, saying, Wherefore hast thou rent thy clothes? let him come now to me, and he shall know that there is a prophet in Israel."*

## 2 Kings 5:1-8 King James Version (KJV)

When it comes to marketing, it is detrimental to look down on anyone. Through a little maid, the ministry of Elisha was celebrated in a far country. That nonentity close to you that you are looking down on may have the keys to an entity. Never look down on any man; they may not be anywhere near your status, but they may know someone who knows someone who has the key to your advancement in life. Value relationships and service them. Just a recommendation can change your life forever, and most recommendations hardly come from highly placed people but from the low- or middle-class people who are strategically positioned in high places.

> *"9 Then spake the chief butler unto Pharaoh, saying, I do remember my faults this day: 10 Pharaoh was wroth with his servants, and put me in ward in the captain of the guard's house, both me and the chief baker: 11 And we dreamed a dream in one night, I and he; we dreamed each man according to the interpretation of his dream.*
>
> *12 And there was there with us a young man, a Hebrew, servant to the captain of the guard; and we told him, and he interpreted to us our dreams; to each man according to his dream he did interpret. 13 And it came to pass, as he interpreted to us, so it was; me he restored unto mine office, and him he hanged. 14 Then Pharaoh sent and called Joseph, and they brought him hastily out of the dungeon: and he shaved himself, and changed his raiment, and came in unto Pharaoh."*

**Genesis 41:9-14 King James Version (KJV)**

Before now, Joseph had served Portiphar for many

years. Portiphar was one of the princes in Egypt next to Pharaoh, and with all that God did for him through Joseph, which he did testify to, he could not recommend him to Pharaoh. Instead, an ordinary butler servant in Egypt was able to bring Joseph before the king. Beloved, you do not need everybody, but you do need somebody and that person is usually disguised and strategically placed, and you need to turn on your sensitivity in order to identify them.

*"14 But the Spirit of the Lord departed from Saul, and an evil spirit from the Lord troubled him. 15 And Saul's servants said unto him, Behold now, an evil spirit from God troubleth thee. 16 Let our lord now command thy servants, which are before thee, to seek out a man, who is a cunning player on an harp: and it shall come to pass, when the evil spirit from God is upon thee, that he shall play with his hand, and thou shalt be well. 17 And Saul said unto his servants, provide me now a man that can play well, and bring him to me. 18 Then answered one of the servants, and said, Behold, I have seen a son of Jesse the Bethlehemite, that is cunning in playing, and a mighty valiant man, and a man of war, and prudent in matters, and a comely person, and the Lord is with him.*

*19 Wherefore Saul sent messengers unto Jesse, and said, send me David thy son, which is with the sheep. 20 And Jesse took an ass laden with bread, and a bottle of wine, and a kid, and sent them by David his son unto Saul. 21 And David came to Saul, and stood before him: and he loved him greatly; and he became his armourbearer. 22 And Saul sent to Jesse, saying, Let David, I pray thee, stand before me; for he hath found favour in my sight. 23 And it came to pass, when the evil spirit from God was upon Saul, that David took a harp, and played with his hand: so, Saul was refreshed, and was well, and the evil spirit departed from him."*

## 1 Samuel 16:14-23 King James Version (KJV)

From an instrumentalist, to an armor bearer and from there to becoming the king, just by a good recommendation from a fellow who might have just sighted David from afar pouring his oil while in the bush watching over his father's flocks. Most great recommendations often come from people we hardly know. I want to encourage you to keep pouring out that oil into those vessels; you never know who could be watching.

You must also develop the skill of speaking for yourself (marketing yourself). Don't close your mouth to the extent of closing doors of opportunities. David had an opportunity to speak for himself, and he was able to convince the king to go to war against Goliath, who served as a direct ticket to his enthronement.

*"33 And Saul said to David, Thou art not able to go against this Philistine to fight with him: for thou art but a youth, and he a man of war from his youth. 34 And David said unto Saul, thy servant kept his father's sheep, and there came a lion, and a bear, and took a lamb out of the flock: 35 And I went out after him, and smote him, and delivered it out of his mouth: and when he arose against me, I caught him by his beard, and smote him, and slew him. 36 Thy servant slew both the lion and the bear: and this uncircumcised Philistine shall be as one of them, seeing he hath defied the armies of the living God. 37 David said moreover, The Lord that delivered me out of the paw of the lion, and out of the paw of the bear, he will deliver me out of the hand of this Philistine. And Saul said unto David, Go, and the Lord be with thee."*

**1 Samuel 17:33-37 King James Version (KJV)**

*Always remember that you will never have another*

*opportunity to make the first impression.* Never let the first opportunity pass, even if they don't directly present themselves to suit your product or services. Always find a way to connect them. David was faced with a real giant who fought real battles all his life, but David was so bold in sharing about his fights with animals to the point that he was able to win the slot to go challenge Goliath. Remember, at the beginning of this book, we addressed the issue of what you have is all you need to get what you want. Don't you forget that. Every great man sees opportunities in every challenge. Never say you cannot. Face it. You can and you will.

*Let's look at marketing from a broader perspective, from the piece "The Role of Marketing in Organizations"*

**– By Timothy Mahea**

In today's world, the role of marketing in organizations is too important to be ignored. Large and small organizations are competing for the same market, and the most innovative and proactive have emerged victors. Today's global economies have realized the importance of small organizations and are increasingly giving them the much-needed support to sustain their growth. As a result, a company's survival is dependent upon its wise marketing efforts, coupled with financial operations among other functions within its structure.

Competition has escalated more than ever, and as major inroads are achieved in the use of technology, the situation is not getting any better. Social media avenues have been intruded by organizations seeking to capture the audience with their product and service offerings. Most of them have indeed attained much success, and customers are more informed than they were a few years back.

Marketing plays an important role in establishing relationships between customers and the organizations offering products to the market. It gives us the confidence to want to try a new product in the market as opposed to situations where the products enter the market without publicity. This makes the marketing function critical in every organization, irrespective of whether the organization is a profit or non-profit centered. Marketing shapes the image of the organization, how people associate with the organizations products or services, and indeed gives people confidence about their products or services.

When it comes to the profit-led organizations, marketing is responsible for the increase in revenue and, by extension, the increase in the organizations profitability. In addition, the function also helps grow the customer/clientele base for the organization. This is especially so when the organization is dealing with more corporate customers and where decisions involve more than one party.

The marketing function is also tasked with branding of the organization, participation in publicity activities, advertising and customer interaction through feedback collection. Every product launch starts with marketing and ends with marketing, whereby the department establishes the needs of the consumers, and after introducing the product, the department seeks to identify whether the customer's needs were met.

Organizations are competing to be at the top of the customer's mind and, at the same time, trying to protect their market share. Marketing is at the centre of creating customer loyalty and customer retention. As a result, the function carries out promotions and campaigns from time to time, and this has been proven as a successful initiative in attracting more customers.

Without marketing, our brands will not be illuminated, and our organizations will be lifeless. Organization's success is not only determined by the prudent application of funds to the various portfolios of investment, but also by the relationship established with the customers, which is a function of marketing.

Here is another great piece that might be useful as well as updated by Nick G. on February 26, 2014, with a focus on online marketing:

It's hard to overstate the importance of marketing. From hot new startups to local stores, every type of business can benefit from the increased sales and heightened brand awareness that a great marketing campaign can offer. Demystify the goals behind your marketing strategy with these 10 important benefits. Simply put, if you're not marketing your business, you're not making progress. No matter how great your product or service is, without any marketing efforts, you're more likely to stand still and be ignored than to move forward and find customers or clients.

Marketing is a broad term, and one that both business owners and consumers are quick to confuse with other terms like advertising and public relations. Try to think of marketing itself as a big umbrella, with fields like direct sales, advertising, and public relations all tactics that make up different parts of your marketing strategy. Some of the world's most well-known and celebrated companies – from Coca-Cola to Apple – have succeeded using two surprisingly simple tactics: making great products and marketing them well.

In many of our courses, like Lean Marketing for Startups, we've covered some of the easiest, most affordable marketing tactics out there for small businesses and online startups. In others, we've covered specialized topics like affiliate marketing and Facebook advertising.

Marketing isn't rocket science, but it isn't necessarily straightforward either. Read on and you'll discover 10 reasons to market your business, as well as helpful tips and educational courses to help you take action and start developing a marketing strategy today.

## 1. Sale. You'll make more sales.

*"No sales, no company." – **Mark Cuban***

When people know your business exists, they're much more likely to become your customers. If your marketing campaigns are doing their job properly, you'll start to see an increase in sales shortly after you get started.

Depending on the type of product or service you sell and the type of marketing you are engaging in, you could start seeing sales after a few days – in some cases, even a few hours. Online advertising platforms like Google Adwords can start sending you traffic – and potentially customers – within minutes of starting your campaign.

By marketing your business online, you can easily

keep track of which campaigns are generating sales and which aren't. Our course, Conversion Optimization, shows you how to track your sales using online marketing platforms like Facebook Ads or Google Adwords and optimize your campaign for maximum sales.

## 2. Communication. You'll increase awareness.

*"More contact means more sharing of information, gossiping, exchanging, engaging – in short, more word of mouth."* **– Gary Vaynerchuk**

Sometimes your best customers might see your advertisements hundreds of times before they buy anything. A lot of people see an ad or online recommendation and, instead of buying straight away, remember the brand name for future reference.

Raising awareness plants your business's brand, its product, and its benefits in the mind of your target audience. By raising awareness through marketing, you'll build a huge audience of potential customers who know who you are, know what you can offer, and know exactly where to find you.

Don't feel bad if your marketing campaigns don't drive increased sales right away, as raising awareness is often just as important. Our course, Startup Attention, is a great resource for developing your own attention-generating engine that powers your business's marketing.

## 3. Abacus. You'll learn your metrics.

*"What gets measured, gets managed."*
**– Peter Drucker**

Whether you're marketing a bakery or an enterprise software company, knowing your metrics is the key to keeping your marketing campaigns profitable. If you can pinpoint exactly how much your average customer is worth, you know exactly how much you can afford to spend acquiring each new sale.

This makes it far easier for you to optimize your bids on marketing platforms like Adwords and Facebook. It also makes it easier for you to optimize your price and profit margin. Basic online conversion optimization tactics can be used to tweak your pricing and keep your product at the perfect profit margin.

Once you've calculated key performance indicators like your cost per acquisition (CPA), lifetime customer value (LCV), or average revenue per user (ARPU), you'll find it far easier to launch other marketing campaigns and optimize them for profitability.

Launch campaigns, get as much data as possible, and trust your metrics. Once you've got the data, you're in the power position to grow your business and increase sales.

## 4. You'll make consumers trust you.

> *"People share, read, and generally engage more with any type of content when it's surfaced through friends and people they know and trust."*
> **– Malorie Lucich, Facebook**

Who do you trust more: your friend or a complete stranger? The more well-known your company becomes, the more people will trust you. The more people trust you, the more likely they are to buy your products and services.

Building trust isn't something that can be done

overnight. Think of the companies that you trust. Generally, the companies we trust the most are the ones we've been exposed to – either through advertising or by doing business with them – for years.

The earlier you start marketing your business, the longer your target audience will have known you. Start early and build a relationship with your target market that forms an image of sturdiness, reliability, and honesty, and people will respond by trusting your business to live up to its image.

There's a reason people pay more for Coca-Cola or Pepsi than they do for a bottle of store-brand cola. They've spent years forming a bond with the brand, and as a result, they trust it more.

Learn more about building a trustworthy brand in Branding: How to Brand Yourself and Your Business.

## 5. You'll build a social asset.

*"One way to sell a consumer something in the future is simply to get his or her permission in advance "* **– Seth Godin**

What could you do with a list of one million

potential customers? As the expert direct marketers love to say, the money is in the list. By marketing your business now, you can build a powerful social asset that you can sell products to tomorrow.

Whether you opt for an email list or a Facebook Page, giving your audience a way to connect with you gives you a powerful platform for selling products and asking your audience important questions.

No matter what your business sells, you can develop a powerful social asset to use for promotions and outreach in the future. Sell shoes? Send users to your Facebook using a creative ad campaign targeted at sports gurus. Sell auto parts? Advertise to local car gurus using Google Adwords and build a powerful promotional list.

Every great business has a social asset that it can market to, in the form of an online database or an offline address book. Start building your social asset today, and in a few years, you could have a powerful list for promoting your products and increasing your sales.

## 6. You'll learn your marketplace.

*"Understand why and how your audience uses technology and then start trying to align your communications efforts."* **– Brian Reich and Dan Solomon**

When you first start your business, your target marketplace can look as vast as the ocean. Once you start marketing, you dive below the surface, and instead of seeing a massive expanse of blue water, you start to see different communities, subcultures, and a huge network of different connections.

Marketing opens your eyes to the reality of your industry. Once you start your own campaigns, you begin to notice what your competitors are doing. This information helps you develop your own campaigns, learn more about your target audience, and get a better feel for your industry.

You also start to learn why customers chose you. By polling your customers, you can learn what drove them to your product. Using tools like Google Analytics, you'll find out which keywords and websites are referring the most customers to you. Using a Facebook Page, you'll discover what your customers love to comment on and share.

Don't keep your head above the water forever. Once you start marketing, you'll see your industry for what it is – a massive network of opportunities that are waiting for you to seize them.

## 7. You'll discover what works.

*"Give them quality. That's the best type of advertising."* **– Milton Hershey**

Have you ever seen an advertisement and wondered how anyone could possibly be persuaded by it? A lot of the best ads look and feel like the worst. By marketing your business, you quickly learn which types of advertisements and marketing tactics are effective, and which ones aren't effective.

There are hundreds of marketing tactics you could use to find customers. From old-fashioned direct mail to search marketing, experimenting with different marketing methods helps you find the ones that work and focus on them.

Stay focused on acquiring data and test, test, test. Our course, Optimization & A/B Testing Statistics, will help you learn how to test different advertising campaigns and marketing methods until you discover the best tactics, headlines, and target audiences for your business.

## 8. You'll develop an 'ideal customer' profile.

*"You can't just ask customers what they want and then try to give that to them. By the time you get it built, they'll want something new."* **– Steve Jobs**

There's a customer waiting out there for every business. Great marketing makes it easy for them to find you. Over time, as you build a database with the information you've acquired from your marketing campaigns, it also becomes easier for you to find them.

Your ideal customer profile includes variables like age, income, location, hobbies and interests, and occupation. Once you've marketed to hundreds or thousands of customers, look at your data and search for patterns and characteristics that you could use to profile your ideal customer.

The more you can learn about the people you're marketing to, the better. Use polls and surveys to learn more about what your customers are looking for and use their data to target your marketing campaigns better. Open Google Analytics and find the regions where your business achieves the highest conversion rate.

Don't build products based on the feedback of your customers – that's a recipe for failure. However, dig deep into the data you generate from your online marketing campaigns and spot trends and details that you can use to hone in on the type of people that matter the most to your business.

Our free course, Market Research Fast Track, breaks down the basics of identifying your ideal customer while you market your business.

## 9. You'll learn how to test and optimize

*"In the modern world of business, it is useless to be a creative, original thinker unless you can also sell what you create." –* **David Ogilvy**

Knowing how to test different headlines, images,

and advertisements is one of the most important skills you can possess. A headline that sounds great in your mind might barely engage your audience, while another that sounds contrived and silly could be the perfect eye-catcher for generating leads and making sales.

If you can't test and optimize, you'll never know which headline is the winner and which is the loser. Some of the world's biggest companies launch online marketing campaigns with hundreds of different images and headlines to be tested, all in order to find the one combination that produces the optimum return on investment.

A/B and multivariate testing sound complicated, but they're surprisingly easy once you've mastered the basics. Our course, Optimization and A/B Testing Statistics, is a great resource for learning more about formulating marketing hypotheses and using real data to find out which are winners and which are losers.

These testing and optimization courses are also great resources for learning how to spot trends and performance indicators in your online marketing campaigns:

## 10.  You'll build a powerful brand

*"A brand for a company is like a reputation for a person. You earn reputation by trying to do hard things well."* – **Jeff Bezo**

Some marketers set out to sell more products. Others set out to build a brand that's easy to remember. The smartest marketers set out to do both at the same time.

The ultimate goal of your marketing campaigns should be to have customers come to you. Big brands like Google and Facebook don't need to remind people that they exist because their customers already know them and trust them enough to make them part of their daily lives.

Branding is what separates your business from your competitors. It's what makes customers choose you instead of someone else. It's your business's style, reputation, and culture all rolled into one. Brands are essential, and without marketing your business, you'll struggle to develop a memorable, powerful brand.

# Chapter 6

# Pay Your Debt

*"7 Then she came and told the man of God. And he said, Go, sell the oil, and pay thy debt, and live thou and thy children of the rest."*

**2 Kings 4:7 King James Version (KJV)**

Debt holds your freedom hostage, keeping you stuck in unwanted conditions. The prophet instructed the woman to pay her debt before she could enjoy her profits. Don't start eating your profits if you haven't started paying off your debts. A borrower becomes a slave to the lender if they fail to repay their debts. This woman was about to lose her two sons to slavery because her husband couldn't pay his debt before he died, and in order for history not to repeat itself, the prophet gave her a strict instruction: *"Go and pay your debt."*

Unfortunately, many people today are no longer

getting help because they have burned their bridges in the past. Nobody wants to have any transaction with anyone who lacks integrity. One of the best ways to prove one's integrity is in one's ability to pay one's debts. Most financial institutions can only consider giving you a loan when they have checked your credit ratings through credit and payment history to see how credible you are for another loan. Do not eat all your profits, pay your debts, and invest some. It doesn't matter whether it's from friends, family members, neighbors, or financial institutions; whenever you borrow, make plans to pay back even before the due date if possible. By so doing, you keep that door open to get more next time.

There are several reasons and benefits why you must pay your debts and, by all means, live a debt-free life and enjoy your life.

Debt is a common fact of life in most developed nations today. According to a report, roughly eight out of ten citizens of developed countries have debts. The report also found that these individuals feel conflicted about their debt. Nearly 70% of respondents said they would rather not have debt, but they see it as a necessity, and a similar percentage feel that loans and credit cards have given them more opportunities in life.

These conflicted feelings reflect the fact that debt can be both good and bad. Good debt is a useful financial tool, helping you to do things that will improve your finances in the long run – such as going to college, buying a home, or building a business. By contrast, bad debt, such as credit card debt, just weighs you down with interest payments while doing nothing to increase your income. This, in turn, makes you more dependent on borrowing to get through the month, trapping you in an endless cycle of debt.

Being stuck in a debt trap ties up your money so you can't do all the things you'd like to do with it. However, its effects are far more than just financial. Over time, the constant pressure of debt can also damage your work, health, and relationships. Freeing yourself from debt can make your life better in just about every way.

# Financial Benefits

*"7 Then she came and told the man of God. And he said, Go, sell the oil, and pay thy debt, and live thou and thy children of the rest."*

**2 Kings 4:7 King James Version (KJV)**

## 1. More Free Income

When you're carrying a lot of debt, the payments on that debt tie up a big chunk of your income. For instance, suppose you have a 30-year mortgage for $200,000 at 4.5% interest. The payments on that mortgage will eat up $1,013 of your income each and every month – and nearly half of that will go toward interest, not building actual equity in the house.

If you can find a way to pay off that debt early, suddenly you'll have more than $1,000 of extra income available every month. That's more than $12,000 each year that you could spend on all the things that matter to you. You could treat yourself to that kitchen remodel you've always dreamed about, devote more money to your favorite hobby, or go on a fabulous vacation each year. By paying off her debt, the widow put more money in her pocket to live and enjoy her life with her children.

## 2. Earlier Retirement

Earlier Retirement Account. Another thing to do with the extra money you save by paying off your debt is to put it into investments. If you're not putting enough into your retirement accounts right now, that extra cash could mean the difference between retiring at 65 or having to work into your golden years. And, if you're already maxing out your retirement contributions, putting the money into other investments could help you reach financial independence and be able to stop working even earlier.

## 3. Less Risk

One of the worst things about being in debt is the risk it brings into your life. If you're already in debt and have no emergency savings to fall back on, you're always just one financial blow away from disaster. A job loss or a major medical crisis could leave you unable to meet the payments on your debt, which could result in:

- Constant calls from collection agencies

- Being sued for nonpayment, and possibly having your wages garnished
- Having your car repossessed
- Losing your home due to foreclosure or being evicted because you can't pay your rent
- Bankruptcy

Being debt-free removes these risks. It gives your budget room to breathe so you don't have to worry about a single unfortunate event ruining your financial and personal life.

## 4. A Better Credit Score

Carrying a lot of debt really weighs down your credit rating. The closer your credit cards and loans are to the limit, the lower your score will be. A bad credit score can cost you thousands of dollars a year in higher interest rates, making it harder to escape from your debt trap.

The flip side of this is that as you pay off your debt, your credit score will improve. This, in turn, can offer a wide range of potential benefits:

- Better interest rates on any future loans
- Lower insurance premiums

- A better chance of landing your dream job, since employers often check credit scores to see if a potential employee is reliable
- A better chance of finding an apartment, since landlords sometimes do the same
- Better deals on cell phone service

## 5. Better Job Performance

Being in debt can also hold you back at work. Worries about money can keep you up at night, which makes you a lot less productive on the job the next day.

If you've reached the point where you have to deal with debt collectors, the problem is even worse. They're likely to call you up at the office, interrupting your work and impairing your productivity. Debt collectors can even contact your employer directly in an effort to locate you – an embarrassing situation that can strain your relationship with your boss.

By contrast, paying off your debt makes your job more satisfying. You feel a lot more motivated to work harder when you get to keep the money you make, rather than spending it all on debt payments. And if you've been stuck in a job you hate because you needed the money to pay those credit card bills, paying off the debt frees you to look for a new job that's more rewarding.

## Mental Benefits

### 1. Less Stress

Less Stress Mental Benefits

Living with debt is a major source of stress. You worry constantly about how you're going to pay all the bills and what could happen if you lose your job. The constant pressure of having to work to pay off debt, while feeling guilty about spending on even the smallest of pleasures, grinds you down.

A 2013 study at Northwestern University found that young adults (aged 24 to 32) with high levels of debt report overall stress levels about 12% higher than the average. Other studies have found even stronger effects. For instance, in the 2001 Life Events Inventory created by the Society of Occupational Medicine, which ranked 100 life events based on how stressful they are, "getting into debt beyond means of repayment" came in fifth. It was rated more stressful than losing your job, getting a divorce, or becoming temporarily homeless.

Getting rid of debt is like lifting a huge weight off your chest. You no longer feel trapped, like you're constantly running in a hamster wheel. You can sleep more easily. And, with your thoughts no longer locked into the constant pattern of worrying about money, you can devote more energy to work, family, friends, and pastimes you enjoy.

## 2. Better Mental Health

Stress isn't the only mental problem that's linked to debt. The Northwestern study found people with a lot of debt were 13% more likely than average to report symptoms of depression. A 2014 study published in The Journals of Gerontology: Series B found a similar effect for adults over 50. In this group, having "unsecured debt" (that is, debt that's not backed by assets, such as a house or a car) had a strong link to depressive symptoms – and the higher the amount of the debt, the worse those symptoms were likely to be.

At its most extreme, debt can even lead to suicidal

tendencies. A 2012 Huffington Post story reports that people struggling with overwhelming student loan debt often struggle with thoughts of suicide, and a few have actually taken their own lives.

The fortunate flip side of this is that being debt-free improves your mental health. You're less likely to suffer from anxiety or depression and more likely to be happy with your life as a whole. A 2014 study at Purdue University found that lower levels of debt play almost as big a role as higher income in people's overall levels of happiness. It's a great feeling to know that you own a car or a house free and clear, and no one can ever take it from you.

## 3. Boosts Self-Esteem

Being in debt can eat away at your self-esteem. Psychologists and debt experts interviewed by Fox Business say people with debt often go out of their way to create a life that looks picture-perfect on the outside – a beautiful house, new cars, nice clothes – because they don't want anyone to know their real financial situation. Of course, all these things cost money, which just makes their financial situation worse and increases their feelings of shame.

By contrast, paying off debt can boost your self-confidence like magic. In the Fox Business article, one woman recounts her experience of buying a new car for the first time after paying off $120,000 in debt. When the car salesman ran her credit check, her initial response was panic – followed quickly by elation as she realized that for the first time, the results would actually be good. This thrill often makes people as eager to share the stories of their escape from debt as they were anxious to hide the debt while they still had it.

## 4. Better Cognitive Function

Debt isn't just an emotional problem. It can actually impair your cognitive function – your ability to think and reason. A 2017 meta-study published in Frontiers in Psychology points to numerous studies showing that experiencing poverty – both in real life and in laboratory conditions – impaired people's attention span, working memory, and self-control.

This is a problem that feeds on itself. Weaker

cognitive function can make you worse at making financial decisions, which can make your debt problems still worse. The Frontiers in Psychology paper showed that financially stressed people were more likely to choose small gains now over much larger ones in the future. They were also less adept at evaluating risks. They were less willing to take risks that could lead to long-term gains, yet more willing to take risks that could lead to long-term losses.

Fortunately, studies also show that paying off debt reverses these problems. A 2017 study at the National University of Singapore offered families with high debt a big chunk of money – equivalent to several months' worth of income – to pay it down. It found that as the participants reduced their debt, their cognitive function rose significantly. They also felt less anxious and became better decision-makers.

# Physical Benefits

## 1. Minimizes Illnesses

The stress debt brings can damage your body as well as your mind. The same Northwestern University study that linked debt to anxiety and depression also found that people with higher levels of debt report worse physical health overall.

Debt can damage your health in a variety of ways. According to psychologist Carole Stovall, one of the experts interviewed in the Fox Business article, stress can be a trigger for heart disease, allergies, gastrointestinal problems, and diabetes. A 2008 survey by Associated Press (AP) and AOL Health bears this out, showing that people with high levels of debt-related stress are more than three times as likely to suffer from ulcers and other digestive problems as people with lower debt stress. They're also twice as likely to have heart problems, including arrhythmias and heart attacks.

Chronic stress can also suppress your immune

system, putting you more at risk for infectious diseases, such as colds. On top of that, money worries can keep you awake at night, further damaging your ability to fight off illness. The AP study found that people with high debt stress were more than twice as likely to suffer from insomnia or other sleep disorders.

When you pay off debt, you can feel better instantly – physically as well as mentally. Those nagging headaches and stomachaches will ease up. And with better sleep and better immunity, you're more likely to escape that nasty virus that's going around at the office.

## 2. Reduces Blood Pressure

Having too much debt can actually raise your blood pressure. In the Northwestern study, people with higher debt showed a 1.3% increase in diastolic blood pressure compared to the average. That may not sound like much, but it's enough to make a real difference to your health. An increase of just two points in blood pressure raises your risk of hypertension (dangerously high blood pressure) by 17% and your risk of stroke by 15%.

This means paying off your debt could do more

than make you feel better; it could actually save your life. A 2016 report from the Federal Reserve Bank of Atlanta on how debt affects death rates found that as people's credit rating improved, so did their mortality risk. An increase of 100 points in credit risk (Equifax's equivalent of the FICO score) reduced the overall risk of death by 4.38%.

## 3. Eradicates Pain

Some studies suggest that debt can even cause physical pain. The 2008 AP survey found that 44% of all people with high levels of debt-related stress suffered from migraines, compared to just 15% of those with lower debt stress. They were also more likely to suffer from back pain and general muscle tension. Another study, published in Psychological Science in 2016, found that people with high levels of "economic insecurity" were more likely to buy over-the-counter painkillers.

Even thinking about financial insecurity, the scientists found, could increase people's pain levels. Subjects who had to think about a financially unstable time in their lives reported almost twice as much physical pain as those who thought about a financially secure period. And since the less debt you have, the less time you have to spend thinking about it, it stands to reason that paying off debt will help ease those aches and pains.

## 4. Better Preventive Care

Most health problems caused by debt are in some way related to stress. However, there's one debt-related problem that's simply a matter of dollars and sense: not being able to see your doctor often enough.

A 2013 study in the Journal of Health and Social Behavior found that people who have high levels of credit card debt or medical debt were less likely to see a doctor or dentist regularly. Even when they were sick, these people often skipped doctor visits because they couldn't afford the bills. (On the other hand, people with "good debt," such as home and car loans, were no more likely to avoid doctor visits.)

So, that's a final way paying off your debt can boost your health: You can always afford to see a doctor when you need one.

# Relationship Benefits

## 1. Promotes Better Relationships

Being in debt stirs up a lot of negative emotions, such as anxiety and depression, fear, and anger. These feelings tend to spill over into your relationships with others at work and at home. When you're worried about how to pay the bills, you're more likely to snap at your spouse or be short-tempered with your colleagues at work. You get mad at your boss for not paying you enough and feel resentful when your friends tell you about their vacations, since you can't afford one yourself.

Getting rid of debt will make you a happier person, and that, in turn, will make your relationships better. You'll be more patient with your spouse, your kids, your friends, and your coworkers. Even new people you meet will like you more when you're not in a bad mood all the time because of debt stress.

## 2. Builds A Stronger Marriage

Money problems, including debt, always put a

strain on a marriage. Even when both partners see the debt as a problem and are working to eliminate it, the stress it causes makes them more likely to be irritable with each other. It can also affect them physically, sapping the energy out of their sex life.

However, when one spouse is working hard to pay off the debt while the other keeps blithely spending, that's a situation that's bound to lead to fights about money – one of the biggest sources of tension in a marriage. The Institute for Divorce Financial Analysts says money problems are the third most common cause of divorce, right after basic incompatibility and infidelity.

The good news is that, when you work through these problems together, your marriage can actually come out stronger at the end. The process of paying off your debt will force you to communicate better, and the experience of surviving a crisis together will create a stronger bond between you. In the case of a married couple, I strongly advise that it must be a mutual effort to ensure both are debt free in order to maintain a healthy marriage relationship.

## 3. Makes you a Better Parent

Paying off debt can make you a better parent in several different ways. First of all, it will free up income that you can put toward taking better care of your kids. If your son needs braces or your daughter wants to take up a sport, you won't go into a panic over where the money will come from. And you can also afford to save for your children's future – for example, by investing for their college education.

Becoming debt-free will also improve your emotional state. The freedom from debt stress will make you more pleasant to be around and give you more energy to devote to playing tag or helping with homework. And because paying off debt strengthens your relationship with your spouse, it will create a better home environment for your kids.

Finally, the process of paying off debt will make you better at teaching your children about money. You can help your children learn from your mistakes by teaching them how to avoid debt in their own lives.

## 4.  **Better position to Help Others**

Getting out of debt has one more big benefit: It makes it possible for you to help out others when they need it. For instance, you can lend money to friends or family members who need it to get through a tough period. If they're struggling with debt, you can also give them the benefit of your experience to help them figure out how to get out. Sharing your success story can inspire others and give them the boost they need to tackle their own financial problems.

In addition to helping out people you know, being debt-free allows you to give money to charity. Happiness economists have found that spending money to help others is one of the most rewarding things you can do with it. It's a great feeling to know your money is helping to make the world a better place.

# In conclusion

Knowing the benefits of being debt-free is one thing, but actually figuring out how to do it is another. Fortunately, there are lots of resources out there that can help. Start by using a debt payoff calculator, such as the one at Credit Karma, to tally up your debts and set a timeline to pay them off. Then create a household budget through Tiller that sets aside a specific sum each month to put toward paying down your debt – and make this the first bill you pay every month, before you start spending on anything else.

Next, look at ways you can hasten your debt payoff. Consider debt snowflaking, which involves looking for little extra sums of cash to put toward your debt each month. If you have multiple debts, look into the benefits of a debt consolidation loan to reduce your interest and simplify your payments. Additionally, consider comparing the debt avalanche and debt snowball methods, which involve allocating all extra money to one debt at a time to pay it off as quickly as possible.

If you're in really desperate straits with debt, try looking for outside help. See if you can negotiate with your creditors to reduce the balance you owe them. Consider talking to a credit counselor about setting up a debt management plan to get your debts paid off in a fixed time frame while avoiding new ones. Do whatever it takes to get that debt out of your life so you can start living fully again.

# Chapter 7

# Enjoy Your Profit

*"7 Then she came and told the man of God. And he said, Go, sell the oil, and pay thy debt, and live thou and thy children of the rest."*

**2 Kings 4:7 King James Version (KJV)**

There are individuals who merely exist but are not living. It is not every rich fellow who makes money and knows how to enjoy it. In order to live a balanced and fulfilling life, you must know how to enjoy your profits. Never put all your profits back into a business without setting aside a portion to enjoy. The feeling you get from eating the fruit of your labor gives you the motivation to work more, so you can enjoy more.

Myra McElhaney is a writer, author, and speaker who encourages others to "Enjoy Life and Do Good!"

Some folks may wonder if enjoying life is really important. Isn't it more important to work hard? Be successful? Serve others? I don't believe so. Here's why:

When you enjoy your life, you spread joy to others around you. Don't you prefer to be around joyful people? Others do, too. Most of us are influenced by the energy of those around us. Joyfulness is contagious. Catch it and spread it!

We only get to live this life once. (As far as we know for sure.) I recently read a story of a man who learned that he had only months to live. He decided to go back and apologize to people he'd hurt and been mean to. The article made me sad for him. How much happier he and others would have been if he had been thoughtful and kind throughout his life, rather than just in the last few months.

Joy gives you energy. When you're happy and enjoying your own life, you get more done because it's easier. (Nope, I don't have scientific proof. Just personal experience!)

> *"13 And also that every man should eat and drink, and enjoy the good of all his labour, it is the gift of God."*

When you enjoy your life, you give others permission to enjoy theirs. It's easy to get caught up in the 'gotta do more,' gotta achieve more,' 'gotta work hard' mentality, especially when we're around others with that mindset. When others see you working and living with joy, they'll understand that they can, too!

The Bible says so! Read Ecclesiastes 3:12, 13. It says,

> *"I know there is no good in them but for a man to rejoice and do good in his life. And that every man should eat and drink and enjoy the good of all his labour, it is the gift of God."*

Do you want to live a happy life? If you say yes, like most people do, then it's important to learn to enjoy life. Some people may think that they can only enjoy life when they already have a lot of money or have a successful career. But that's not true. You can enjoy your life where you are with what you already have. You can enjoy your life now.

Here I will share with you how to enjoy life. But before that, I'd like to share a few tips that are essential for living a happy life.

## 1. Be Grateful

*"16 Rejoice evermore. 17 Pray without ceasing. 18 In everything give thanks: for this is the will of God in Christ Jesus concerning you."*

### 1 Thessalonians 5:16-18 King James Version

I can't emphasize enough how important this is. No matter how many pleasant things you do, if you don't learn to be thankful, you will always see things negatively. Gratitude magnifies your strength and helps you celebrate your little wins.

Practice gratitude daily. You don't just need to find new ways to use things you already own; you can find ways to think more positively about your current situation.

Challenge yourself to 21 days of daily gratitude...

This can take whatever form best suits you – you can journal and jot down things you're grateful for throughout the day, you can share your thoughts with a loved one and bounce ideas off each other, or, of course, you can keep your thoughts to yourself.

Either way, you'll be making a huge step toward

enjoying your life in new ways. After the classic 'shelter, food, safety, health,' you may hit a bit of a wall.

Dig deeper and start thinking about other aspects of your life that really matter to you.

It may be that you love being a regular at your local coffee shop, and it feels good that the barista always knows your order. It may be something like having the time to take your dog for a walk after work – or even just having a dog!

Whatever you choose, focus on the feeling it gives you. After the first week or two, you'll find it super easy to think of things you're grateful for.

## 2. Do Not Rush Things

> "20 *A faithful man shall abound with blessings: but he that maketh haste to be rich shall not be innocent.*"

### Proverbs 28:20 King James Version (KJV)

Life has a lot of simple things you can enjoy. But if you move too fast you will overlook most of them. So don't be in a hurry. Don't move too quick. Slow down and pay attention to the world around you. Most of the ways I'm about to share will work well only if you slow down.

## 3. Be Content

> *"5 Let your conversation be without covetousness; and be content with such things as ye have: for he hath said, I will never leave thee, nor forsake thee."*

**Hebrews 13:5 King James Version (KJV)**

Lack of contentment is the root cause of envy, hatred, and many malicious activities that result in a sorrowful life. It is good to be challenged and motivated by your neighbor's achievements in life, but never let them make you undermine your own achievements.

Life is pretty great, most of the time! The problems arise when we overthink and start comparing our lives to those of others.

It can be hard to focus on what we have in our lives when we're bombarded with edited images of people 'living their best lives.'

Social media can encourage feelings of inadequacy and low self-esteem. We live in a world of filtered photos and unrealistic expectations, which can make it very hard to live in the moment and see things for what they really are.

If you want to enjoy your life more and in new ways, it's worth considering how often you just let yourself relax into the moment and appreciate what's really happening.

I am not suggesting that you completely give up on social media, but try to change your perspective a little bit to enjoy what's actually in front of you.

Of course, it's unrealistic to try to do this every minute of the day – we all have unpleasant thoughts and feelings crop up from time to time!

However, if we stop thinking about how our lives should look and what we should be doing and instead focus on what our lives are like and what we are doing, we'll be well on the way to feeling more content.

> *"11 Not that I speak in respect of want: for I have learned, in whatsoever state I am, therewith to be content."*

**Philippians 4:11 King James Version (KJV)**

Contentment is the first weapon you need to overcome difficult situations. For you to learn to value and appreciate life, you must learn to be content. Always bear in mind that no matter how bad your situation may appear at times, you are still better than somebody.

Enjoying life doesn't need to mean adding new things to it. Sometimes, it simply means falling back in love with what's already in it.

Think about things that you already own that aren't being used to their full potential. Thinking about new hobbies will sometimes remind you of things that might be buried away and forgotten about.

It's more common than you'd think – most of us have a camera stashed in a cupboard somewhere, and a pair of roller-skates tucked away in the garage!

Rather than buying new things each time you fancy injecting some excitement into your life, consider what you already own and find ways to maximize their use.

This will help you feel better about your life – you'll feel resourceful, crafty, and you'll essentially be getting something 'new' for free. It's a win-win situation.

*"⁸ And having food and raiment let us be therewith content."*

**1 Timothy 6:8 King James Version**

Once we learn to be in the moment, we can move on to being happy. Sometimes, we need to give ourselves permission to be happy.

It might sound strange, but a lot of us hold back from letting go. Accepting where we are in our lives and learning to enjoy it takes a lot of effort and energy.

We all hold back for different reasons. Some of us are scared to admit that we're happy with the way things are because we worry that we'll 'jinx' it.

We don't want to commit to a relationship because we don't want to let ourselves get too attached or reliant. We're scared to say that we love our job just in case it gets snatched away from us.

This is quite natural and is a form of protection against any future pain we fear might arise.

By accepting that change is inevitable, we can find

ways to make the most of what we have now and let ourselves sit back and unwind.

Once you push past the fear of clinging to things for safety, you can enjoy them for what they are and be happy.

This will help you enjoy your life like never before and will shift the way you view other things, too.

## 4. Stay Away From Unnecessary Drama

*"17 Now I beseech you, brethren, mark them which cause divisions and offences contrary to the doctrine which ye have learned; and avoid them."*

**Romans 16:17 King James Version**

Let's be honest – there have been times in all of our lives when drama has been entertaining.

Sometimes it's quite fun to have lots going on and it can be a great distraction from your real life.

And, sometimes, that distraction will become your worst enemy. Drama can be incredibly toxic and can steer our minds in a very negative direction.

It may seem relatively harmless at the time, but it's

likely to have a much deeper impact than you may initially realize. It may be unintentionally dragging someone else down, or will be shining a negative light on your own life.

Avoid this type of behavior and you'll feel so liberated!

As soon as you let go of the mentality of complaining about other people or talking down your own actions, you'll feel so reenergized.

You'll get to a stage where those around you seem petty for gossiping, and that's okay – rise above it and get on with your own life.

By shifting the focus from other people's drama to your own reality, you can get stuck into enjoying your life like never before.

## 5. Acknowledge And Celebrate Your Wins

*"19 And out of them shall proceed thanksgiving and the voice of them that make merry: and I will multiply them, and they shall not be few; I will also glorify them, and they shall not be small."*

## Jeremiah 30:19 King James Version (KJV)

One of the reasons a lot of us don't reach our full 'happiness potential' is that we're too busy focusing on what's **not** happening in our lives.

God increases you when you learn to celebrate your small wins.

It can be very hard to monitor our own progress at times, especially if we're feeling stagnant in our job, relationships, or personal life.

Part of not enjoying life to the fullest comes from feeling like we aren't very 'good' at it.

This is where self-assessment comes in. Write down things about your life you want to change or aren't content with. This can be anything that comes to mind, from not being able to quit smoking to feeling bored at work.

List it all down and set yourself some goals – but be realistic and specific. Instead of 'quit smoking,' choose something like 'buy patches and gum; listen to hypnotherapy tape' and think of ways you can help yourself.

If you're quite pressure-oriented, give yourself a deadline. Set an alarm on your phone to check the list in a month's time and see how well you're doing with your goals.

It may be that after a month, you've not bought any patches and haven't taken any steps toward what you want to achieve. Do not despair!

Sure, you've not done what you set out to do, **but** this can work as a great motivator – do you want to check this list again in another month and have the same feelings of disappointment crop up?

If you **have** checked these things off your list, celebrate. Not with a cigarette, of course!

> *"⁵ When a man hath taken a new wife, he shall not go out to war, neither shall he be charged with any business: but he shall be free at home one year and shall cheer up his wife which he hath taken."*

**Deuteronomy 24:5 King James Version**

The scripture permits you to take a break from work and enjoy your achievements no matter how small they are.

Give yourself the credit you deserve and make a note of how great you feel for doing what you said you'd do.

Being accountable to ourselves is important in terms of self-esteem, so you deserve to feel good about it.

This will also remind you how great it feels to achieve things next time you set yourself goals – it's all about positive reinforcement.

## 6. Explore Life

*"37 And she said unto her father, Let this thing be done for me: let me alone two months, that I may go up and down upon the mountains, and bewail my virginity, I and my fellows. 38 And he said, Go. And he sent her away for two months: and she went with her companions, and bewailed her virginity upon the mountains."*

**Judges 11:37-38 King James Version (KJV)**

Get out of your comfort zone and into something exciting. You can explore somewhere you already know, you don't need to go abroad for an adventure!

Grab a camera and wander around your local town – you'll be amazed at how many more things you see when you're paying attention.

Something that many people experience in terms of not enjoying life is that feeling of being 'stuck,' of being in a stale place in their lives.

This is totally natural and happens to all of us at some point, and there are some easy ways to deal with it.

If you've been living in the same place for some time, it's no surprise that you feel like there is nothing new for you. By getting out and physically exploring, your mindset will start to shift and you'll start actively looking for new things.

It could be something as small as floral decorations cropping up in community flower beds, or a new coffee shop on the other side of town.

It's important to note that these new things don't have to be life-changing; they just need to remind you that change is happening all around you.

Think about the seasons and the way they affect the landscape of your home. Use the shifting seasons to shift your mentality to one of positivity and openness, and you'll be surprised by how many things you notice and how refreshed you start to feel after each excursion.

## 7.  Attempt Something New

> *"19 For I am about to do something new. See, I have already begun! Do you not see it? I will make a pathway through the wilderness. I will create rivers in the dry wasteland."*

### Isaiah 43:19 New Living Translation (NLT)

The only way you can see the new thing God is doing around you is when your mind is open to trying new things.

God is a god of new beginnings. Enjoy life more by expanding what you fill it with. Try new activities – lots of places offer a free trial, so you don't need to pay or commit before you're ready.

It's worth looking into community classes or online courses; you'll be amazed at what you can find. Go for something physical and enjoy an energy boost, or choose an academic course online.

YouTube is a great resource, with thousands of videos to get you motivated into trying out a new hobby, as well as advice and support when you've started.

If you're after new tricks and hacks for your camera, get online and find some tutorials. Or follow other people's journeys as they try Pilates or kickboxing for the first time – it's always great to know you're not alone in those achy muscles!

If you can afford to splash out slightly more, travelling opens up a whole world of adventure and new experiences, and will give you a new take on your own life – we'll get onto this later on.

## 8. Take Care Of Your Body

*"8 For bodily exercise profiteth little: ..."*

**1 Timothy 4:8 King James Version (KJV)**

Your body needs that little profit for you to stay

healthy and enjoy life.

Part of 'living your best life' and enjoying life to the full is looking after your body.

Sure, we all know that we should be eating lots of fresh fruit and veg, drinking plenty of water, and exercising regularly.

It's so easy to acknowledge these aspects of healthy living and shrug them off, but it's important to create space for them in your life.

By shifting your mindset and physical routine, you'll start to see things differently – you may be more capable of doing active things like family bike rides, or you may gain clarity in terms of your mentality through meditation.

Either way, treating your body like a temple isn't such a bad idea after all! Yoga and meditation can have a profound impact on your life, even if you only practice them sporadically.

Eating well and staying hydrated will help you enjoy life more because you'll be energized and functioning much better.

This will impact your attitude toward work, relationships, and friendships, all of which have a huge knock-on effect on your happiness and enjoyment levels.

By working out or taking steps to incorporate more exercise into your life, your body will let you do so much more than you think it's capable of.

However you choose to make a change, you'll see a big shift in your enjoyment levels of life in a very short time!

## 9. Love And Appreciate Yourself

*"31 And the second is like, namely this, Thou shalt love thy neighbour as thyself. There is none other commandment greater than these."*

**Mark 12:31 King James Version (KJV)**

You cannot love others if you haven't loved yourself enough. You can only give what you have.

Take time to do what makes you feel good. It might sound simple, but it'll open a gateway to enjoying life on a whole new level.

As we've already discussed, we can be so harsh on ourselves – it is true that we're our own toughest critics. Comparing ourselves to those around us and what we see on social media can be very damaging.

All of this combined can lead to a toxic cycle of punishment – we get frustrated with ourselves for not being as 'good/fit/successful' as others and push ourselves into relentless activities to try to 'better' our situation.

This might mean staying after work for hours on end, forcing our weary bodies through grueling workout sessions, or creating a negative mental health space by constantly blaming ourselves.

These might sound like common actions or *re*actions, but they are not healthy. A lot of us wind up punishing ourselves rather than working to improve ourselves – and there is a huge difference in those two things.

Rather than beating ourselves up, we have to learn to be kind to ourselves and acknowledge that we are growing and changing constantly.

By doing this, we can spend time and energy looking after ourselves and filling our lives with positive things that we enjoy.

Ironically, the more comfortable we are in our personal lives and the more we do things we enjoy, the better we feel about ourselves – and the more likely we are to improve at work, want to be healthier, and be more committed to our passions.

Everything will fall into place as soon as you start caring about yourself and let go of the blame you're crippling yourself with.

## 10.   Don't Be Rigid

*"10 And whatsoever mine eyes desired I kept not from them, I withheld not my heart from any joy; for my heart rejoiced in all my labour: and this was my portion of all my labour."*

**Ecclesiastes 2:10 King James Version (KJV)**

We know – conflicting advice! There are times when planning can help you get the most from life, and times when letting go will serve you so much better.

We all know the saying 'live every day like it's your last,' but it's not all that realistic – for one, you'd probably quit your job!

Rather than throwing caution to the wind, we'd recommend lightly sprinkling a little bit of caution into a gentle breeze.

Plan where you need to – anything to do with your job, children, and financial situation, for example, needs to be taken seriously.

By mapping out these areas of your life, you'll be set up for long-term success, and you can relax in the present and be content in the knowledge that you've future-proofed your life.

This can help you enjoy life even more as you don't need to worry too much about things that are far away.

That said, there are areas of your life where you need to learn to let go a little bit – this will really push you into a new level of life-loving!

This is where travelling, exploring, and learning new skills all come into play. Think about the aspects of your life where you can afford to relax and then go for it.

Planning everything can make us quite miserable, and it gets very boring knowing exactly what our life is going to look like.

By finding that balance between sensibility and spontaneity, you'll open yourself up to so much more enjoyment.

With those few tips in mind, here are a number of simple ways to enjoy life. Pick the ones that work for you:

- Enjoy your meal. Don't just eat. Taste it and appreciate its richness.
- Learn to cook.
- Feel music and not just listen to it.
- Play music. More than just listening, playing music allows you to express yourself.
- Sing.
- Gather with old friends.
- Take a walk in the park.
- Go hiking.
- Read a novel.
- Find and watch a movie you like. IMDB's

recommendation engine can help you find movies you may like.

- Give yourself a lazy day.
- Play board games with your friends.
- Have a candle-light dinner with your spouse.
- Play mini games.
- Read comics.
- See beautiful pictures.
- Read inspiring quotes.
- Learn to paint.
- Read a classic book.
- Exercise with friends.
- Watch funny videos.
- Play with kids.
- Play a mind game.
- Have a cup of coffee.
- Get a massage.
- Go to a museum.
- Go to a theater.
- Watch sunrise.
- Take pictures.
- Browse your photo album for your treasured memories.

Beloved, you are not just born to add to the number of people existing on earth. You are born to live and make an impact. Stop limiting yourself and thereby limiting the power of God at work in your life. The widow limited herself, allowing her circumstances to control her response to life, and by doing so, she limited her manifestation. The world is waiting for you to manifest, and my aim is to encourage you to do so. What you have is all you need. So, rise up today, shake yourself from the dust, pick up your broken pieces, take it one step at a time, and keep moving till you get there.

There is a limitless power at work in you; stop limiting the limitless YOU.